THE MAN WHO PLEASES

AND

THE WOMAN WHO CHARMS

Also Called:

The Art of Attraction

BY

JOHN A. CONE

"Look out lovingly upon the world and the world will look lovingly in upon you."

TO
MY MOTHER.

CONTENTS.

PREFACE.

The makers of books have been divided into two classes—the creators and the collectors. In preparing this volume the author has made no claim to a place in the first division, for he has been, to a great extent, only a collector. The facts which the book contains are familiar to intelligent people, and the only excuse offered for presenting them in a new dress is that we need to be reminded often of some truths with which we are most familiar.

In our daily intercourse with one another, we may forget to render to others that thoughtfulness and attention which we exact from them.

We all know that the essence of courtesy is the purpose, in speech and manner, to be agreeable, attractive, and lovable, to awaken by our presence happy impressions in another. We all understand this, but we so easily forget it, or, at least, forget to put it into practice.

Courtesy is not the least of the Christian virtues, and it should be studied as an art.

The reader is requested to accept these chapters in the spirit in which they were prepared. They are not profound psychological studies, or even original essays, but only a bringing together of simple, yet important truths, which are of concern to us all. Possibly they may be of some help—"Lest we forget,——"

THE MAN WHO PLEASES.

The dearest friend to me, the kindest man,
The best-conditioned and unwearied spirit
In doing courtesies.

Merchant of Venice.

He hath a daily beauty in his life.

Othello.

Such a man would win any woman in the world if a' could get her good will.

Much Ado About Nothing.

There are few subjects of deeper interest to men and women than that of personal fascination, or what is sometimes called "personal magnetism." We commonly talk about it as though it were some mysterious quality of which no definite account could be given.

"A man is fascinating," we say, "he is born magnetic; he has an indefinable charm which cannot be analyzed or understood," and, with the term "naturally magnetic," we hand the matter over to the world of mystery.

Is this quality of so bewildering a nature that it cannot be understood, or will a study of those men and women who possess preëminently the power of pleasing show us the secret of their influence, and prove to us that the gift of fascination is not, necessarily, innate, but that it can, to a great degree, be acquired?

Will we not find that what appears to be the perfection of naturalness is often but the perfection of culture?

From all our well-known public men who have won the reputation of being "naturally magnetic," perhaps we could not select a better example than James G. Blaine. With the possible exception of Henry Clay, no other political leader in our history, under all circumstances, had so devoted and determined a following. Both Clay and Blaine possessed sympathetic and affectionate dispositions, and both understood human nature and the art of pleasing. It may be said that Mr. Blaine's popularity was due, in a great measure, to the brilliant and attractive nature of his public service, and this was, no doubt, true to a certain extent. No man knew better than he the importance of making the most of opportunities for dramatic and sensational display, and his methods of statesmanship were always calculated to please the multitude.

His greatest power, however, was manifested in his winning men by direct and individual contact. One thing which assisted him in this direction was the fact that he was, perhaps, the most courteous of all the public men of his generation. Whenever a stranger was introduced to him, a hearty handshake, a look of interest and an attentive and cordial manner assured him that Mr. Blaine was very glad to see him. If they chanced to meet again, after months or even years, the man was delighted to find that Mr. Blaine not only remembered his name, but that he had seemed to treasure even the most trivial recollections of their short acquaintance. He had a marvellous memory for faces and names, and he understood the value of this gift.

This ability to remember faces is not difficult to acquire. We could all possess it if we would make sufficient effort. No two figures or countenances are precisely alike, and it is by noting how they differ one from another that you will remember them.

In explaining his own remarkable memory for faces, Thomas B. Reed once said to a reporter that he never looked a man in the face that some striking peculiarity, a line, a wrinkle, an expression about the eye, the set of the lips, the shape of the nose, something set that man's face down in his mind indelibly, and distinguished him from the rest of mankind.

Blaine carefully trained himself to pick out some feature or peculiarity by which he could distinguish one face or person from all others and by which he could associate the name of the individual.

The ability to remember names and faces is one of the most valuable accomplishments for the man in public life, or, indeed, for any man or woman who wishes social success. Not only does it insure comfort to one's self, but it is especially pleasing to others. Next to the comfort of being able to address by name and without hesitation a person one has met but once, and without mistake, is the comfort of being recognized one's self.

Another reason why Mr. Blaine was popular with the masses was because he was not difficult to approach, and he never missed a chance to be useful to a person who might some time, in turn, be useful to him.

The *St. Louis Globe-Democrat* said shortly after his death: "It was not the habit of Mr. Blaine to wait for men to seek favors from him. He anticipated their desires, and doubled their obligations to him by doing voluntarily what might have been delayed for solicitation. That gave him the kind of popularity which outlasts defeat and resists all ordinary influences of criticism and hostility. He could always count upon a certain measure of unflinching and unconditional support, whatever forces happened to be arrayed against him; and he changed bitter enemies into zealous friends with a facility that was a source of constant surprise and wonder."

But why should his success in attracting others to himself be a source of "surprise and wonder"?

Mr. Blaine, in common with many other magnetic men and women, understood that the secret of personal fascination lies in one single point; that is, "in the power to excite in another person happy feelings of a high degree of intensity, and to make that person identify such feelings with the charm and power of the cherished cause of them."

Any quality, good or evil, that enables a man to do this, renders him fascinating, whether he be saint or sinner. Indeed, some of the men who have been the most skilful in the art of pleasing have been scoundrels.

Said a writer in the *Boston Herald*: "It used to be said of Aaron Burr—so irresistible in charm of manner was the man—that he could never stop at the stand of the ugliest old crone of an apple-woman, without leaving on her mind when he went away the conviction that he regarded her as the fairest and most gracious of her sex. And so, had woman suffrage prevailed in his day, he would have had the solid vote of the apple-women for any office he might aspire to."

Aaron Burr clearly understood that the woman does not exist who is wholly without sentiment, and he always appealed to that part of a woman's nature.

He understood very well the truth of these words written by Croly: "In the whole course of my life I never met a woman, from the flat-nosed and ebony-colored inhabitant of the tropics to the snow-white and sublime divinity of a Greek isle, without a touch of romance; repulsiveness could not conceal it, age could not extinguish it, viscissitude could not change it. I have found it in all times and places, like a spring of fresh water, starting up even from the flint, cheering the cheerless, softening the insensible, renovating the withered; a secret whisper in the ear of every woman alive that to the last, affection might flutter its rosy pinions around her brow."

Burr, understanding this, left in the mind of the apple-woman the firm impression that he thought she must have been at one time a duchess, reduced in fortune by some accident, and now driven to the last refuge of an apple-stand, and that those sad facts evidently accounted for the traits of high breeding and delicate refinement so visible through all her present poverty.

He understood the fact that all people live in two distinct worlds—the world of reality and the world of imagination. In the world of reality they use brooms and shovels, wash floors and dishes, or sell apples; in the other, they live in drawing rooms, feast sumptuously and are the wonder and admiration of mankind.

"Few people," continues the writer in the *Herald,* "would believe that an ugly, dilapidated looking apple-woman could dwell in the enchanted realm of imagination just as much as the rich and favored do. But Burr believed it, so when he spoke to the old crone, he went up, not to her withered and beggarly self, but to her ideal self, imaginatively entering into the duchess dream in her, and instinctively became deferential in his bearing.

"Forthwith the duchess in her came out to meet the courtly gentleman in him, and greetings were exchanged as between two incognito scions of noble lineage. Each enjoyed the meeting, each had vividness enough of imagination to impart to it the flavor of reality, and to keep out of sight common, material facts."

"But," you say, "not every man can make such an impression, for few are able to do and say things with the ease and grace of a Burr. There must be a naturalness of manner which never suggests suspicion. Let the average man attempt to force his nature and to manufacture smiles and looks of pleasure, and the old apple-woman will know at once that she is being fooled." Very true, and it is not desirable that the average man should possess the ability of an Aaron Burr to influence others. Few persons try as he did to acquire that power, but because the average man cannot at once exercise that potent influence over others which he did, it does not follow that we are unable to understand the secret of Burr's success, nor is it evident that other men cannot acquire something of this power by thinking it worth while to do so.

It would not be safe to say that all men can be equally successful, try as they will, in inspiring in others "happy feelings of a high degree of intensity," for nature has not been impartial in bestowing equally upon all the gifts of adaptation and expression.

There are a few persons so constituted by temperament and mental organism that they exercise a depressing influence over their associates. They have a negative, flabby spirit that seems to operate, speaking figuratively, much as a wet shoe does upon one who is compelled to wear it. They draw upon the nervous strength and exhaust the patience of those who are compelled to be much in their company. But there are not many of this type. Most of us could make far more progress in acquiring social graces and in the art of pleasing than we do.

Let us now consider some of the particular qualities which render a man pleasing to the opposite sex.

Of course different types of men please different women. Some women care little for the moral element in men. They do not admire them for their goodness or nobility of character, but rather for their manners and their ability to flatter and say pleasing things. Some women are fascinated by mere brute strength, but they are not many. Rank, wealth, and social position are very attractive to some, but these things do not make the man himself more attractive to the true woman.

While a girl is young, she may go into raptures over "a cameo profile, a Burnes-Jones head of hair, or a pre-Raphaelite languor and pallor," but these things are bound to pall, and become absolutely distasteful. Some even admire downright wickedness in men, and these are the women who send delicacies to murderers in prison, and overwhelm them with bouquets. But, fortunately, these types represent but a small fraction of the fair sex, and this chapter has to do only with the great majority; the intelligent, moral, cultured women of the land. What qualities in men are most attractive to them?

Physical beauty is always attractive in either sex, yet the handsome man has the advantage of his plainer rival only in this—he is able to draw attention to himself at once. He must, however, have something more to hold that attention. He may be physically an Apollo, but if he be ill-mannered, dull or ignorant, he will stand no chance beside the man skilled in the artful polished ways of what is called society, who is master of that grace of manner and flexibility of speech which more than wealth, reputation, or personal attractiveness, win their way with women.

It has been proven, again and again, that even ugliness of face and form is not, by any means, a bar to popularity with women, and while we are often amazed at the choice which brilliant, beautiful women sometimes make from a crowd of admirers, at the bottom of every apparent fantastic selection, there is a solid, and, usually, a sensible reason.

Ernest Renan was certainly not handsome. He was exceedingly corpulent, his complexion was said to resemble nothing else so closely as tallow. He had claw-shaped hands, bushy gray eyebrows, and thin gray hair, yet wherever he went into society he was sure to be the center of an admiring group of women. He was not fascinating by reason of his ugliness, but in spite of it. There was enough in the subtle charm of his manner, and the melodious flow of his conversation, to make up for all outward deficiencies.

Liszt was not a handsome man—quite the contrary; yet probably no other man ever lived who exercised a more magnetic and potent influence over women. Even when he had become gaunt and old, his eyes dim, his blonde hair snow-white, his spare, lean figure wrapped in a black, priestly gown, he was followed about by a train of fair admirers.

Chauteaubriand could charm at eighty-four, the Abbé Liszt at seventy-five, and Aaron Burr—who was by no means handsome—had at seventy a charm of manner that was irresistible.

The fact is, one cannot recall half a dozen very talented men who were admired for their personal beauty. Pope was very plain; Dr. Johnson was no better; Mirabeau was "the ugliest man in France," and yet he was the greatest favorite with the fair sex.

These examples are not cited to prove that women do not care for physical beauty in men. On the contrary, that is a very strong attraction, but not the most powerful factor in holding them. Women more frequently prize men for their sterling qualities of mind than men do women. A perfection of physical beauty rarely associates itself with great mental ability in either sex, but still there have been some notable exceptions, especially among women, and every pretty woman who reads this may consider herself one of these exceptions.

As a general thing, the man who pleases is the man who understands. It does not matter much to a woman whether a man has great and brilliant thoughts of his own, if he comprehends her wishes and her feelings, as well as her thoughts. He should, if he desires to please, make a careful study of that mysterious and complex thing—a woman's nature. He must understand that it is of a finer fibre than his own; that it is sensitive and easily hurt. He should have sentiment, but not be a sentimentalist. He will be wise, indeed, if he can skilfully draw the line between the two things. "Sentiment is divine: sentimentalism absurd." He should be able to say much in little and he must not be a chatterer. A woman who talks too much becomes tiresome; a man who is an aimless talker is an intolerable bore to both sexes.

Few men understand a woman. They do not look at things from her point of view, and, therefore, do not realize to what extent civilized life has permitted her to assume that convention of manner and those civilities of speech which are in some harmless degree hypocritical. It could not be otherwise. Her ideal of a man is a very high one, but she rarely meets him, and so she accepts the one who comes nearest to her ideal and makes the most of the situation. She would that he were different, but a woman can love in spite of very many things. Usually she is obliged to if to love at all. She is much cleverer at love-making than a man. "She is an artist where he is a crude workman, and she does not go through a love scene without realizing how much better she could have done it if the title rôle had been given to her."

If she is a woman of sensibility, she is shocked by a hundred disagreeable habits which many men think justifiable. She is repelled by awkwardness of manner, coarse modes of speech, by carelessness of person and dress, and yet, for all that, she loves.

The lover who is most successful in retaining the affection of a sweetheart or a wife is the one who expresses over and over again the love and the tenderness he feels. Women, more than men, like to hear things talked about. They are far more wide-awake to the value of trifles, and more sensitive to changes of mood. They are given to saying in many ways, with delicate variations, what a man is satisfied to state once for all, even to state badly.

A man will believe in a woman's love and be satisfied with far fewer visible tokens of it than are necessary to confirm his tenderness and keep her convinced of it.

The truth is that a man's power of pleasing does not depend upon some occult quality of which no account can be given, but upon the degree in which he holds certain attractive qualities—innate or acquired. We have no difficulty in understanding any single one of these qualities, yet when a man possesses such a combination of them as to entitle him to the term "fascinating" we pronounce it incomprehensible, and fall back upon that vague term, "personal magnetism."

The personal elements which are most conducive to our influence over others are, in a broad way: good manners, a pleasing voice, the ability to converse well, personal neatness, taste in dress, tact, good morals, culture and refinement, physical beauty, and intellectual force. We are pleasing or offensive just in proportion to our possession of these very desirable characteristics, and, possibly, what we term "personal magnetism" is simply the result of a well-balanced development of some, or all, of these enviable characteristics.

THE WOMAN WHO CHARMS.

Look on this woman. There is not beauty, not brilliant sayings, nor distinguished power to serve you; but all see her gladly; her whole air and impression are healthful. Manners require time, as nothing is more vulgar than haste.

Emerson.

Possessed with such a gentle, sovereign grace,
With such enchanting presence and discourse.

Comedy of Errors.

She's a most exquisite lady.

Othello.

Is it the handsome woman? Yes, sometimes, but not always. Beauty is always attractive, but the handsome woman has the same advantage only that the handsome man possesses—she draws attention to herself at once. If she has nothing but her beauty to rely upon, she does not hold the attention.

It was Balzac who reminded us of the fact that nearly all of the most celebrated attachments in history were inspired by women in whom there were noticeable physical defects. Mme. de Pompadour, Joanna of Naples, Cleopatra, La Valliere—in fact, almost all the women whom a romantic love has invested with a halo of interest—were not without imperfections and even infirmities, while nearly all the women whose beauty is described to us as perfect, have been finally unhappy in their loves.

"Perhaps," says Balzac, "men live by sentiment more than by pleasure. Perhaps the charm, wholly physical, of a beautiful woman has its bounds, while the charm, essentially moral, of a woman of moderate beauty may be infinite."

Whether this be true or not, women surely overestimate the influence of mere physical beauty to attract and hold men. Madame de Staël, whose dominion over the hearts of all those with whom she came in contact is well known, declared that she would gladly give up all her gifts of person, and all her learning, if she could receive beauty in exchange. It was fortunate for her that her wish was not granted, for, had it been, probably she would have found her kingdom slipping away. While she did not have a beautiful face, she possessed physical characteristics and personal traits which rendered her absolutely fascinating.

To a sensible man nothing is quite so insipid as a vain, brainless, tactless beauty, whose opinions are but echoes, and who imagines that her beauty alone will hold him chained to her chariot.

Beauty holds for a time, but after a man's eyes are satisfied, he must be entertained, and the plain girl who possesses brains and tact need have no fear of her more beautiful rival. Modern research has proved that not Sappho, not Aspasia, nor even Cleopatra were women who would have attracted any special attention by reason of their physical beauty. Their highest charm was intellectual—the possession of an "immensity to give," as Plutarch expresses it, in the way of grace and accomplishment.

The idea that plain girls are allowed to run to waste as "unappropriated blessings," is not supported by evidence, for we are constantly meeting wives far plainer than the majority of the unmarried women of our acquaintance; and it frequently happens that a man who has a wife physically beautiful, becomes enamored of an exceedingly plain woman who possesses a certain quality of congeniality, some trait of adaptability which he misses in his partner.

Says a writer in *Lippincott's*: "It is safe to make the broad generalization that a homely girl, all other things being equal, is likely to have fewer offers than a pretty girl, but quite as likely to receive the one offer which will make her a happy wife. But all other things (save the gift of beauty) seldom are equal between the homely and the pretty girl; by the natural law of compensation, the homely girl has either some inherent or some acquired ability that is lacking in the other, which asserts its charm as acquaintance progresses. Beauty only has the start in the race."

It frequently happens that the beauty makes the mistake of expecting to be entertained by her admirers, and does not exert herself to please. The plain girl, however, is often superior in tact, for being obliged to study human nature closely in order to get the most out of companionship, she learns to depend upon this knowledge in her efforts to please. She is not dazzled by admiration, nor is she unduly confident when she obtains it that she will retain it.

Mme. Hading, who is a strikingly handsome woman, and, therefore, can discuss beauty without falling under suspicion, once said:

"A woman is very unfortunate who has nothing but beauty to insure her success. There are other things superior to beauty. Taste, good taste, brains, tact, health, those are the things a woman must have to hold people. And then there are good manners—so rare and yet so easily cultivated. To be refined, to be gentle, to be amiable, to be charitable in thought and in speech, to be intelligent, is to be charming, in spite of an unattractive body and an ugly face. To be well born is, indeed, to be blessed, but to rise above low birth is sublime. The greatest painter of the age could make only a caricature of a face for the Empress Josephine, and yet the sweetness of her smile and the charm of her pleasing and gracious ways immortalized her name. There are other ends to happiness than mere wealth; there are sweeter things in a woman's face than beauty."

Again, the woman who charms is not necessarily young. History is full of accounts of women who have been fascinating when beyond middle life. The truest and strongest love is not always inspired by the beauty of twenty. The enthusiasm over sweet sixteen is not supported by the old experience which teaches that the highest beauty is not found in immaturity. Louis XIV. wedded Mme. Maintenon when she was forty-three years old. Catherine II. of Russia was thirty-three when she seized the Empire of Russia and captivated the dashing young Gen. Orloff. Even up to the time of her death—at sixty-seven—she seemed to have retained the same bewitching power, for the lamentations were heartfelt among all those who had ever known her personally.

Cleopatra was considerably over thirty when Antony fell under her spell, which never lessened until her death, nearly ten years later.

Livia was thirty-three when she won the heart of Augustus, over whom she maintained her ascendancy until the last. Aspasia did not wed Pericles until she was thirty-seven, and for more than thirty years after that she was regarded as one of the most fascinating women of her time. Ninon de l'Enclos, the most celebrated wit of her day, was the idol of three generations of the golden youth of France, and she was seventy-two when the Abbé de Berais fell in love with her.

Helen of Troy, the celebrated Greek beauty, was over forty-five when she took part in the most famous elopement in history; and as the siege of Troy lasted ten years, she must have been at least fifty-five when the ill-fortune of Paris restored her to her husband, who is reported to have received her with unquestioned love and gratitude. Mlle. Mars, the celebrated actress, was most attractive at forty-five, and Mme. Récamier was at the zenith of her good looks and of her power to please when between thirty-five and fifty-five. Diana de Poitiers was over thirty-six when Henry II., then Duke of Orleans, and just half her age, became attached to her, and she was regarded as the first lady and the most beautiful woman at court up to the time of the monarch's death and the accession to power of Catherine de Medici.

The common idea that the mature beauty of forty is less fascinating than that of the girl of seventeen or eighteen is without foundation. By beauty is not meant merely well-formed features and a fresh complexion—these things even dolls possess. In spite of the rosy, fresh complexion bestowed upon youth by nature, a woman's best and richest age is really between thirty-five and forty-five, and sometimes considerably beyond that period.

No one would dare say how old Madame Patti is. Everyone who meets her exclaims at her marvellous youthfulness and vivacity. Patti's explanation of her bright eyes, smooth skin and happy expression is given in a few words: "I have kept my temper. No woman can remain young who often loses her temper."

As a woman grows older, she ought to become more attractive in certain ways than she could be in her youth. One of the most needful things for attaining this result is good health. Fine muscles, a healthy, glowing skin, eyes bright with energy and ambition—these make a valuable foundation for the woman who would be attractive. The woman who, at a certain age, considers herself *passé,* commits a great error. If she so regards herself; if she believes she has passed the time when she can be interesting, others are quite likely to find her unattractive. Surely a woman should be more interesting after she leaves the period of girlhood. She ought to be able to converse better, she should possess more wisdom, greater tact, broader knowledge of human nature; and she should have more repose, more grace of manner. Indeed, she should have all her accomplishments well in hand, and be more facile in their use for the pleasure of others; and she will be able to use them to better advantage if she has cultivated placidity of temper, human sympathy and generosity, and is not careless of her personal appearance. It frequently happens that women who have reached middle life neglect many of the aids to physical beauty which they once carefully followed. They are careless about dress, and grow to esteem it excusable to dispense with those simple and necessary accessories of the toilet which formerly helped to make them so exquisitely fresh and dainty. They grow accustomed to think that untidiness must necessarily be associated with drudgery. But in these days it is becoming more possible to carry the element of refinement and beauty with us everywhere.

Many women could seem much finer, more delicate than they appear, if they were not accustomed to think that a certain homeliness, and even negligence of attire is quite excusable, and, indeed, almost inseparable from common work-a-day life. As we grow older, it becomes more necessary that we use care in always presenting that appearance of personal neatness which never fails to be attractive to those with whom we come in contact.

One of the strongest elements a woman can possess to attract the other sex is a sympathetic interest in a man's work. This was what attracted Dr. Schliemann, the famous Greek scholar and explorer, to the young woman whom he married. She was familiar with the Iliad and the Odyssey, and was an enthusiast upon the subject of uncovering the ancient cities of Homer.

Men like to have women interested in the things in which they themselves are interested.

One who has read Richard Harding Davis' "Soldiers of Fortune" may remember that Clay grew very fond of Miss Langham. His first disappointment in her came to him when he discovered her lack of interest in his work of opening up the iron mines in South America. Miss Langham's younger sister, Hope, was, on the other hand, extremely interested in the mines, made an exhaustive study of the methods of mining, and when she, with the other members of the family, visited the scene of Clay's engineering operations, it was she who drew Clay's attention to herself by intelligent questions and suggestive remarks. He was delighted with her, admired her, fell in love with her, and then married her. That day at the mines was the beginning of the end of the old love, and the awakening of the new.

To interest men a woman should, by reading the papers, acquire, and be able to express, a reasonably clear idea of what is happening in the world. She should ascertain what is of special interest to the particular man she wishes to attract, and, whether the subject be politics, business, out-door sports, art, science, or literature, she should be able to contribute something in a conversation upon that subject more interesting than a mere yes or no.

As it is the manly man who wins and satisfies a good woman, so it is the womanly woman who pleases and retains the regard of the estimable man.

Men like the womanly woman. She need not be soft or silly, weak or nervous; she may be strong, vigorous, resolute, and brave. A man has little sympathy for the girl who imitates men either in dress, manner or conversation. If a womanly man is not pleasing to either sex, what shall we say of a manlike woman!

He thoroughly expresses the writer's view who said: "A perfect woman may be adorable; a woman who is perfect would be beyond endurance." Yet, however irreligious a man may be himself, he always dislikes irreverence in a woman. He wishes and expects his wife to be better than he is, and, generally, she is.

Men do not like the over-dressed woman—the one who goes to the extreme of a fashion and a little further. He does not care for costliness of apparel, but he is always attracted by freshness and daintiness.

A sense of humor is a valuable gift in a woman who wishes to please. Men like the girl who sees the funny side of a thing; who can make them laugh; who can be witty without being sarcastic; who can jest and not be malicious; who can relate humorous experiences without saying things calculated to make others uncomfortable.

A man likes a woman who entertains and amuses him. Young girls often express surprise that one of their number is so popular among men. They know she is not so pretty as dozens of other girls. She is not dressed so richly as they are, yet, at a party, she will have half a dozen young men about her while they are neglected and alone. She must, they conclude, have that indefinable quality of magnetism, and that is all that can be said about it, and they could not find out the secret if they tried. But probably there is no secret about it. Although she is not pretty, and does not possess a vast amount of information, she has tact, and a quick and electric vivacity of spirit which acts as a breeze on the sluggish waters, making ripples of pleasure and laughter, and so produces an exhilarating effect upon all about her.

Many young men, if diffident or awkward, feel, it may be, a little out of place. They hardly know what to do or say, but this particular girl wakes them up, and they find themselves laughing and talking with astonishing ease. She understands how to make them feel at ease, how to draw them out, and as they associate with her they become unusually elated, and it is not at all strange that in every company they look eagerly for her presence.

While, judging from the descriptions and representations which we have of her, Cleopatra was by no means beautiful, there is no mystery about her fascinating influence over men.

"She had," said a writer in *The Boston Herald*, "jaded Roman conquerors to deal with, men sated with every form of mere animal pleasure. There was no piquancy left in anything; all had palled and staled on their cloyed palates. But in Cleopatra was evermore something fresh, unexpected, perfectly original!

"No wonder the bystanders cried, 'Age cannot wither nor custom stale her infinite variety.' What had she to fear from the rivalship of mere youth and beauty so long as her nimble intellect was fertile, like the Nile floods, in successive harvests, in the one quality her lovers were ready to lavish kingdoms for, namely, 'infinite variety.'"

To go back to the definition of personal fascination given in the preceding chapter, we repeat that it consists "in the power to excite in another person happy feelings of a high degree of intensity, and to make that person identify such feelings with the charm and power of the cherished cause of them."

There may be such a thing as the "indefinite quality of magnetism" which draws people to the possessor whether they will or no; but there are many personalities who are charming because they have willed to be, because by painstaking perseverance they have acquired those characteristics which enable them to please and charm all with whom they come in contact.

THE ART OF CONVERSATION.

"*Though conversation, in its better part,*
May be esteemed a gift and not an art,
Yet much depends, as in the tiller's toil,
On culture and the sowing of the soil."

Cowper.

In all countries where intelligence is prized, a talent for conversation ranks high among accomplishments. To clothe the thoughts in clear and elegant language, and to convey them impressively to the mind of another, is no common attainment.

Mrs. Sigourney.

The man or woman who is an intelligent, tactful conversationalist, commands one of the most essential elements of a pleasing address. While all of us may have certain defects which we cannot wholly overcome, however earnestly we may try, we can, if we will, re-form our conversation. We can so train ourselves that good nature, considerateness and benevolence will always have a place in our intercourse with others. We can, if we will, use good English, and we can avoid the temptation, so common, to talk of persons rather than of things. Theoretically, we despise gossip; practically, most of us add our mite to the common fund. We may not be ill-natured, and the sweet charity that "thinketh no evil" may have a home in our hearts; yet sometimes, if we are not watchful, it may fall asleep, and bitterness, or the spirit of spitefulness come creeping stealthily to the surface.

We can, if we will, be intellectually honest—a kind of honesty which is indeed rare. The principal reason why arguments and discussions lead to so must dissatisfaction and ill-feeling on the part of the disputants, is the lack of this quality.

Two men are engaged in conversation and a question of religious belief or of politics is brought to the front. Each takes a side in the discussion and maintains his opinions to the end. Neither is searching for the truth, but is eager to defend his side of the question against the attacks of his opponent. It does not occur to either that anything else can be the truth except the things he has been taught to believe. To both, the truth simply takes the form of their own opinions; and since they are most firmly attached to their opinions, neither ever questions his own devotion to the truth. Such persons can scarcely be said to use their minds at all, for their thinking has been done by some one else. Many a hostess is obliged tactfully to separate aggressively argumentative and disputatious guests, who have never learned that others have an equal right to their own opinions, and that not every dinner party is the proper occasion to plunge into heated argument in the hope of changing another's views.

Again, we can all avoid the habit of exaggeration—a fault which does not get itself called by the name of "falsehood," but which is in dangerously close proximity to it. A man hears something, true enough in its original shape, but he passes it on with a little addition of his own. The one to whom he tells it adds his touch of exaggeration, until, at last, the statement is so swollen and distorted as to convey anything but the real truth. It would be difficult to charge any one with deliberate prevarication. The result is a sort of accumulative lie, made by successive individual contributions of little dashes of exaggeration. Thousands who would never be guilty of inventing an entire story derogatory to the reputation of another, are constantly contributing to the formation of these accumulative falsehoods, which are quite as evil in their results as though conceived and concocted by one person.

We can put into requisition a nice sense of honor in our conversation. In a hundred different ways this most fitting attribute of the true woman and the real gentleman is often put to the test. We can remember that it is quite as easy to be ill-mannered in speech as in conduct.

There are men and women who, at a dinner, would not under any circumstances, transgress the rules of table etiquette, but who may offend quite as grossly by a thoughtless or an intemperate use of words. They may not dispense with the fork, but they wound the heart by unkind words. They may observe all the amenities from oyster-fork to finger-bowl, yet they offend some member of the company by sarcasm or personal innuendo. They may not misplace or misuse the napkin, but they may render the entire company uncomfortable by declining to yield, in argument, to the greater weight of evidence; or by overloading a story with unimportant details. They may be scrupulously neat, and of easy and graceful deportment, but may never have learned the gentle art of keeping one's temper sweet when criticised or when confronted by a contradiction.

These very suggestive words appeared in "The Churchman": "It is almost a definition of a gentleman to say that he is one who never inflicts pain. The true gentleman carefully avoids whatever may cause a jar or a jolt in the minds of those with whom he is cast. He has his eyes on all his company; he is tender toward the bashful, gentle toward the distant, and merciful toward the absurd. He avoids unreasonable allusions on topics which may irritate; he is seldom prominent in conversation, and never wearisome. Another delightful trait in him is that he makes light of favors when he bestows them, and seems to be receiving when he is conferring. He never speaks of himself except when compelled, never defends himself by a mere retort. He has no ears for slander or gossip; is scrupulous in imputing motives to those who interfere with him, and interprets everything for the best. He is never mean or small in his disputes, never insinuates evil which he dare not say out. He has too much good sense to be affronted at insults, and is too well employed to remember injuries. He may be right or wrong in his opinions, but he is too clear-headed to be unjust. He is as simple as he is forcible, and as brief as he is decisive."

The entertaining talker is not, of necessity, a great talker; he is often a good listener. He understands that a bright story, briefly told, will amuse, but that people are bored by a long story, filled with pointless details. He is not necessarily learned or profound. He understands that small change is of as much importance in social intercourse as it is between men in business. "Although deprecated by some wise people as vain and frivolous," says *Zion's Herald,* "small talk has a legitimate function in human intercourse. It is the small coin of conversation. Those who despise its use often get on as badly in social life as would the merchant who should exclude the dimes and quarters from his money-drawer. Without them, the wheels of trade would be blocked. An honest old copper penny will often turn the corner of a good bargain. Chit-chat gives ease to conversation. The strait-jacket is removed; the mental forces have full play; the man acts himself; and the communication of soul with soul becomes free and delightful. With small talk he is familiar, and can toss it about as a juggler does his cards. The philosopher with his learned and exact phrases at once deadens the flow of soul."

Men and women are not strictly original. The things we say to-day have been said just as well a thousand times before; but that forms no reason why we should not say them again. The coins in your purse have been through a hundred hands and are not the less useful in serving you again.

The fellowship enjoyed rather than the store of wisdom communicated, is the end of conversation. Whether they say anything of importance or not, we like to hear some persons talk; they inspire us and set our own mental machinery in motion. Small talk often brings us most readily in contact with another soul.

All good conversationalists know the use of small talk. To be sure, they know something more, something larger and better, but the chinks in the larger subject are filled in wonderfully by a familiar interpolation of the smaller things in a chatty way. Many a wise and learned man would be a better talker if he had at hand a supply of small coin. He can talk extremely well on serious and recondite subjects, but the quick jest and easy repartee of the parlor and the dining-room are beyond him. He is, in spite of his learned lore, at a disadvantage in society, where there is no time for homilies or for treatises on erudite topics. Persons less gifted chat and laugh and have a good time while he sits in gloomy silence. Those who would please and be pleased in social intercourse must carry with them and be ready to dispense the small change of light and witty conversation.

To be popular in society, find out whether your companion prefers to talk or listen; avoid personalities;

endeavor to lead the conversation to subjects familiar and interesting to others rather than especially pleasing to yourself; never indulge in sarcasm; be good-natured and sympathetic; strive to be tactful; exchange small courtesies; talk to all with equal attention and interest, and whatever the topic of conversation, or wherever you may be, appear cheerfully contented. Acquire, and then exhibit, that adaptability to place and people which conduces ever to grateful and pleasing companionship.

William Mathews writes in *Success*: "Conversation rules the destiny of the state and of the individual; from diplomacy, which is essentially the art of conversing skilfully on political themes, down to the daily transactions of the mart and the exchange, its empire is evident to all.

"Such being the potency and importance of conversation, why is so little attention given to its culture to-day? Why is it that so many educated men, who are fastidious regarding their personal appearance, and bestow upon their bodies the most solicitous care, are yet willing to send their minds abroad in a state of slovenliness, regardless of the impression they make?"

GOOD ENGLISH.

We should be as careful of our words as of our actions.

Cicero.

An accomplishment, in its accepted meaning, is "something acquired which perfects or makes complete; an attainment which tends to equip in character, manner, or person, and which gives pleasure to others."

Surely, then, the man or woman who desires to please cannot possess too many accomplishments; and, accepting the definition just given, is there any other accomplishment of greater importance than facility in speaking and writing one's native language with ease and with elegance? Is there any other single test of culture so conclusive as this? Is it not the matter, and, particularly, the method of one's speech more than anything else which impresses the person whom we meet for the first time, either favorably or unfavorably in regard to our acquirements? We may have but few opportunities during a lifetime to display our knowledge of geometry, algebra or astronomy; we may be for weeks in the company of other people without giving them an opportunity to suspect that we possess any knowledge of Latin or Greek, but as long as we live, and every day we live, we are giving evidences of facility or awkwardness in the use of our mother tongue.

How much time is wasted in practicing upon unresponsive musical instruments—unresponsive because not touched by sympathetic fingers! How much time is spent in acquiring a slight knowledge of French and German, which results, generally, in an ability to use a few simple phrases, and to translate easy sentences with the aid of a dictionary! How many young women, with no artistic ability whatever, spend weeks and months under the instruction of teachers in vain attempts to produce something in oil or in water-color worthy to be called a picture! How much more to the advantage of these young women would it be if a part of this time were spent in acquiring a better understanding of the use of English!

The writer once knew a girl who, after playing a selection upon the piano, left the room and burst into tears because she had been guilty of a slight blunder in her execution—a blunder not noticed by two of the twenty persons assembled in the parlor. This same girl, however, exhibited, habitually, a carelessness in pronunciation, and an ignorance of English grammar of which she should have been heartily ashamed, and which caused far more annoyance to her friends than her blunders in music.

Boys and girls should be trained to feel that it is as discreditable to them to confound the parts of speech in conversation, as it is to make discords in music, or to finish a picture out of drawing, or to be guilty of some inadvertence of manner. They should be made to feel that proficiency in music, French, German, or painting, or any other accomplishment, so-called, will not compensate for slovenliness of diction.

In addressing a girl's school, Bishop Huntington once said: "Probably there is not an instrument in common use, from a pencil to a piano, which is used so imperfectly as language. If you will let me be plain, I suspect that it would be safe to offer a gold medal as a prize to any young lady here who will not, before to-morrow night, utter some sentence that cannot be parsed; will put no singulars and plurals in forbidden connections; will drop no particles, double no negatives, mix no metaphors, tangle no parentheses; begin no statement two or three times over without finishing it; and not once construct a proposition after this manner:

"When a person talks like that, they ought to be ashamed of it.'"

These are frank statements to address to a class of young ladies; but the Bishop's implication would hold with equal truth not only in the case in point, but also with a large number of the high schools, seminaries and colleges of this country. Surely such a charge against the other practical branches of study could not be made and sustained.

When James Russell Lowell said: "We are the most common-schooled and the least educated people in the world," he might have added that the statement was especially applicable to our habits of using or abusing our mother tongue.

This general indifference to good English is not, in most instances, the result of a lack of knowledge, for time enough is devoted to the study of technical grammar in almost all schools, to enable the pupil to become thoroughly acquainted with the principles which govern the use of our language.

It is because many persons, not having acquired the habit of correct speech, do not think to apply the rules of grammar in conversation. Were children accustomed from infancy to hear only correct English, there would be but little need to memorize arbitrary rules of grammar, for they would, from habit, speak and write correctly. Thus it is that the children of educated parents are generally so easy and graceful in their conversation, contrasted with the children of the uneducated. Our language, like our manners, is caught from those with whom we associate.

Several other nations are far in advance of our own in the thoroughness with which their youth are drilled in the use of language.

In France, a knowledge of the French language, spoken and written, is regarded as of special importance. In all entrance examinations, or examinations for promotion or graduation, the pupil's knowledge of his native tongue is first determined; and no promotions are allowed, and no diplomas granted, if the student is notably deficient in this regard, even though his knowledge of the other required branches should prove to be all that could be desired. We have not so high a standard in the United States. It has been but a few years since a definite knowledge of English was added to the requirements for admission to American colleges, and even now it has not, in any of our educational institutions, the relative weight in determining examinations which French and German have in the systems of those countries. While great improvement has been made in teaching English, and while better methods are employed than formerly, it is still safe to say that in no other branch of study, pursued with equal diligence, are the results so unsatisfactory.

Surely in no other way do we so clearly show the degree of our culture and refinement as by our every-day conversation. Is it not important, then, that we devote our efforts seriously, and with infinite patience, if necessary, to mastering a matter so essential?

The selection of good English does not necessarily imply either a stilted monotony of speech, or a tiresome affectation. It is simply elegance and naturalness. There is no reason why any person, however humble his station in life, should not hope to speak his native language correctly. It is an accomplishment which is not expensive. In its acquirement one does not require high-priced teachers. It demands only care and attention. Be critical of yourself. Watch your sentences. Get your companions to correct your slips of the tongue. Say over correctly the troublesome sentence until the mistake becomes impossible. Listening to well educated persons and reading the best literature are both of great assistance in this direction, especially if we offer to both the sincere flattery of imitation. Our literature teems with masterpieces of style. To read them consistently is to imbibe a certain facility of diction.

There are many persons who, while they do not violate the rules of technical grammar, habitually indulge in slang, hyperbole, and in many "weeds of speech" which should be pulled up promptly and cast aside. A great many boys and girls, and even some older persons, imagine that the use of slang lends piquancy and force to their conversation. Slang is always an element of weakness. It is bad enough in a man, but in women it is far more questionable. It is not the expression of the refined. To the cultivated taste it is discordant.

Another fault prevalent among girls is the habit of hyperbole. Perfectly, awfully, nice, and splendid, are the four most overworked words, and awfully is the most abused of them all. It is strange, the hold this word has secured in the vocabulary of girls who, in almost all other respects, are considerate in their use of English. Persons are called awfully good, awfully bad, awfully clever, awfully stupid, awfully nice, awfully jolly and awfully kind. It is made to do duty on all occasions and under all circumstances, as though it were the only adverb admissible in good society. Among adjectives, splendid easily ranks as the most popular. To many, everything is splendid, whether it is a flower, a sunset, a dinner, a football game, a friend, a sermon, or a book. Then we are continually hearing that certain things are *perfectly* splendid, *perfectly* lovely, *perfectly* hateful, *perfectly* glorious, *perfectly* magnificent and *perfectly* sweet. How word-stricken society would do without these expressions it is difficult to determine, yet certain it is that the woman who deals recklessly in superlatives demonstrates forthwith that her judgment is dominated by her impulses, that her opinions are of doubtful reliability, and her criticisms valueless.

In a recent number of one of the popular magazines Prof. Brander Matthews has an article on the prevailing indifference in regard to the proper use of words. The points which he emphasizes are these:

The gentleman is never indifferent, never reckless in his language. The sloven in speech is quite as offensive as a sloven in manner and dress. The neat turning of a phrase is as agreeable to the ear as neatness of person is to the refined taste. A man should choose his words at least as carefully as he chooses his clothing; even a hint of the dandy is not objectionable, if it be but a hint. It is even better to go to the extreme of fastidiousness than to indulge the opposite extreme of negligence.

The art of writing letters is but another phase of the same matter. Indeed it is but conversation carried on with the pen, when distance or circumstances prevent the easier method of exchanging ideas by spoken words.

It is an art which should be faithfully cultivated by those who desire to please. In social life, in business, in almost every other circumstance of life, we find our pen called into requisition. Yet while it is an almost indispensable accomplishment, it is one which is pitifully neglected. The art of letter-writing is becoming obsolete; that is, the art of writing such letters as enriched the epistolary literature of a former generation. This is unfortunate, as there is nothing that will so stimulate thought, and bring into activity, practical, every-day niceties of phrase as the exercise of this art. Constant drill in letter-writing will tend to take from one's vocabulary words which have no place there, and will accomplish quite as much as any other means to broaden, beautify, and to refine the language at our command, as well as to train the mind to exact habits of thinking. A further important consideration is the charm which "a gem of a letter" has for the delighted recipient.

The indispensable requisites of a good letter are neatness of chirography, simplicity, and grammatical correctness. Defects in any one of these particulars are scarcely pardonable. We cannot all be pretty writers, but we can all write legibly and give to the page the appearance of neatness. Scribbling is inexcusable.

"A scribbled page points to a scribbling mind, while clear, legible handwriting is not only an indication of clear thinking, but a means and promoter of accurate thought. Indeed, simply as a business proposition, one cannot afford to become a slovenly penman."

"And who," says *The Philadelphia Record,* "does not know the charm of a gracefully worded, legibly written letter, with its wide margins, its clear, black ink and dainty stationery? An art, indeed, is the writing of such a missive; an art which it behooves every woman to cultivate. A hastily written line betraying signs of carelessness, and scrawled on an indifferent sheet of paper is a poor compliment, indeed, to the receiver, and elicits anything but flattering comments upon the writer."

Careless speech is quite bad enough, but the charm of the speaker may be so great as to disarm criticism. The letter, however, the written word, stands on its own merits; "what is writ is writ." There is no graceful vivacity to plead for the writer; no coquetry of manner to distract the glance of the reader from the errors coldly set forth in black and white. Observe, then, the utmost care in inditing an epistle, whether to a friend or foe or to a lover. Never send forth a letter in undress, so to speak, scarcely more than you would present yourself *en dishabille* before your most formal acquaintances. The one is almost as flagrant as the other.

TACT IN CONVERSATION.

"Ask only the well about their health."

Discretion in speech is more than eloquence.

Bacon.

Brilliancy in conversation is to the company what a lighted candle is to a dark room—it lightens the whole of it. But every now and then some unskilful person, in attempting to clip the wick to make it brighter, snuffs it out.

James C. Beeks.

Seldom does there occur in society any lapse so astonishing as the uncomfortable remarks innocently made by men and women to each other. Some persons who are careful and considerate in other respects, seem to have a woeful lack of that quality which we call tact. They wish to be pleasing; they would not for the world intentionally say or do anything to injure or wound the sensitiveness of a friend; yet they are continually saying those "things that would better have been left unsaid."

Harper's Bazar mentions some of these speeches which have no excuse for being.

"What a dear little fellow that is!" said a caller to the mother of a three-year-old.

"He is a great comfort to us," replied the mother, stroking the child's long curls.

"Yes; I should think so. He is not pretty, is he? His hair is so beautiful now that at the first glance one would call him pretty. But if you imagine how he will look when those golden curls are cut off, you will see that he will be a very plain child."

Said another woman to an acquaintance: "Mrs. A., I hope you will pardon me for saying that I think I never saw a more beautiful piece of lace than the flounce on the gown that you wore to the Assembly Ball last week. I said to my husband afterward that if Mr. A. should fail again and lose everything, as he has done once or twice already, you could sell that lace and easily get a good price for it."

The same woman, while making a visit of several weeks, said to her hostess, as the time of her departure drew near: "I always think that the nicest thing about making a visit is the returning to one's home. One's family are always so glad to see one, and there is always great luxury to me in getting back to my own house, where I can do what I please, say what I please, and order what I want to eat."

Again, there are people who seem to think that it is their mission to puncture every person's infirmity with whom they come in contact. They study to speak disagreeably. They corner you in the social circle, and talk about the subject they know to be most disagreeable to you, and talk in a tone sufficiently loud to be heard by all the other persons in the room. If you have made a blunder they reveal it. If you have been unsuccessful in any of your undertakings they are sure to inquire about it, even to details. They unroll your past and dilate upon your future. They put you on the rack every time you meet them and there is an instinctive recoil when you perceive their approach.

"We all know these persons," says *Zion's Herald*, "the persons who always utter the unsuitable word, who make themselves generally disagreeable, who never, apparently, try to make a pleasing impression upon others, but who delight to sting and wound."

Are we not all acquainted with the neighbor mentioned in this quotation: "As a brief and sharp tormentor, as a nail in the boot, a rocker for the shins on a dark night, or a sharp angle for the ulnar nerve, Mrs. R——, our neighbor, excels all persons I ever saw. I am quite sure if she could disturb a corpse by whispering to it that its shroud was ill-fitting, and the floral gifts were not what had been expected, she would do it."

If you are a woman have you not more than once gone out for a walk with some other woman who is never satisfied with your appearance?

She gives your gown a pull, saying: "This dress never did fit you; it isn't at all becoming to you, why didn't you wear your other one?" You soon begin to feel uncomfortable, and to wish you were at home again.

Your bonnet may be never so becoming, or your new jacket may fit you to perfection, but she never mentions either. She notices only defects; she sees all that is disagreeable. Such persons always leave an uncomfortable feeling behind them when they leave you.

Sarcasm is not a quality to be cultivated by either sex. Men do not like it in women. It may be amusing when it is directed against another, but there is always a lurking fear that it may some time be directed against one's self. Sarcasm is a rank weed, that, once sprouted, grows and grows, choking out the little plants of kindness, forethought and consideration, until it overruns the garden of the mind, dominating and controlling every thought with a disagreeable, pungent odor that cannot be eradicated.

The sarcastic girl is not fascinating, for she is not a pleasing companion. She is too sharp to be agreeable. She may possess talent above the average of her acquaintances; she may be able to talk in half a dozen different languages; she may be as beautiful as a Greek statue; but men fight shy of her. Sarcasm is not wit, though wit may be sarcastic. One may be bright and say all manner of clever things without hurting the feelings of others by keen, knife-edged opinions that are full of bitterness and teeming with gall.

The tactful person does not make the mistake of talking too much about himself. While we are young, at least, we are very interesting to ourselves, and we are likely to imagine that all the world is interested in our opinions, prejudices and tastes. But though this may be true of our dearest friends, it is not true as far as other people are concerned.

"Without question," says the *Magnet,* "our conversation must be based upon what we have experienced in one way or another. But that does not make it necessary for us to talk continually about ourselves. If we should examine carefully the things we say to the merest acquaintances, we would be astonished, oftentimes, to see that we assume an interest in ourselves which we have no right to expect." People who are ill are likely to make indiscriminate claims upon sympathy, entertaining strangers as well as friends with detailed descriptions of their latest symptoms, and the doctor's latest remedies. Some of us who have not the excuse of illness, impose on the persons we meet by obliging them to listen to a great deal of personal information which may be of interest to ourselves, and possibly to those who love us very dearly, but scarcely to any one else.

Several years ago the *Christian Union* related this incident: The social occasion was a dinner. One of the guests was a woman who had passed middle life; good taste, ample means, with womanly grace and natural refinement, made her an addition to any circle. The hostess of the occasion was a woman who prided herself on her ability to meet the requirements of her station. She had no doubt as to her fitness in any social capacity, but her friends had not the same unquestioning faith in her tact.

The gentle guest found to her delight that she was assigned to the care of the son of an old school friend, and inwardly thanked her hostess for the consideration and thoughtfulness which made it possible for her to hear from her friend, whom she had not met in years. The guests were no sooner seated at the table than the hostess leaned toward the young man, and, in a voice perfectly audible to the entire company, said: "Never mind, Bob, I will do better for you next time."

For one minute there was perfect silence, the lady and her escort alike appalled by what had been said; but the kindliness of the guest overcame the embarrassing moment by calling the attention of the young man to the roses on the table, which, she said to him with a smile, were great favorites of his mother when she was in school. This broke the ice. The hostess was perfectly unconscious that she had been guilty of any rudeness. Her intention was to be particularly polite to the young man; first to assure him that he would be her guest again, and, secondly, that she would then have a rosebud to assign to his care. The amusing part was that the young man greatly admired his mother's friend, and had frequently been her guest on his visits to the city.

It is difficult to imagine how a woman could move in society to any extent and remain capable of such a blunder, and yet we have all passed through similar experiences at the hands of people whose social experience should render such tactlessness impossible. There comes to mind now an imposing woman, who prided herself on the fact that she always said just what she thought. At a reception, she filled the room by her manner; it was impossible to continue oblivious of her presence.

Bowing affably to her acquaintances, she sailed—for women of this type do not walk—up to a modest little lady whose health, she had heard, was declining, and in a loud voice exclaimed: "What have you been doing to yourself? You have aged fifteen years since last I saw you!" Not unkind by intention, she was but practising her system of saying just what she thought, and she was constantly urging upon her friends the propriety of this course; but what an unbearable place our world would be if we all followed this example of inane and inconsiderate bluntness.

So the woman who is always finding in you resemblances to some other person whom she has met, creates many of the uncomfortable experiences of social life, and when she thinks it interesting to exploit the character of your prototype, dwelling upon the mental and physical defects, she becomes unbearable. Yet society has, as yet, found no sure way to eliminate her.

Such infelicities are not the outcrop of unkindness so much as of a certain ineptitude or lack of *savoir faire*. Such people feel constrained to do their share of the talking, but have not acquired tactfulness in selecting the topic, nor alertness to avoid the pitfalls—both of which traits may by sedulous self-training be acquired by any one in whom, unhappily, they are not innate.

In one of these instances bad manners were the natural expression of the woman, because her impulse was selfish; for it is certainly true that a person of truly unselfish nature will not offend by making personal remarks. Manners are the expression of the heart, and the man or woman who lives mentally in kindly, thoughtful relations with fellow men and women will refrain from expressing the thought which might possibly give offence. There is no mystery in social grace. It is remembering other people in their several relations to us. The woman who is a social success is not the one who has for her purpose in life so much the desire merely to please, but the one whose desire, rather, is to make others happy. One is a polite purpose; the other is a fine type of unselfishness that makes impossible the utterance of unwelcome truths to the chagrin of anyone encountered in the casual personal contact that we term society.

Holmes gave us some good advice when he said: "Don't flatter yourselves that friendship authorizes you to say disagreeable things to your intimates. On the contrary, the nearer you come into relation with a person, the more necessary do tact and courtesy become."

THE COMPLIMENT OF ATTENTION.

"Were we as eloquent as angels we should please some people more by listening than by talking."

"A good listener is as needful to a witty talker as steel to flint. It is the sharp contact of the two which makes the sparks fly."

There are certain amenities attending social intercourse with which we are all familiar, yet we are constantly forgetting to put them into practice. In no respect is this forgetfulness more noticeable than in conversation, and especially in connection with what may be called "the compliment of attention."

If you despair of becoming a good talker you can, at least, make yourself a good listener, and that is something not to be despised. There are apt to be more good talkers than good listeners, and, although to say so may sound paradoxical, the better you listen, the greater will be your reputation as a conversationalist.

In the opinion of the cynical Rochefoucauld, the reason why so few persons make themselves agreeable in conversation, is because they are more concerned about what they are themselves going to say, than what others are saying to them.

If you have read "Nicholas Nickleby," you remember Mrs. Nickleby tells how remarkable Smike was as a converser. She entertained poor Smike for several hours with a genealogical account of her family, including biographical sketches, while he sat looking at her and wondering what it was all about, and whether she learned it from a book or said it from her own head.

Said a writer in the *Chicago Herald*: "What is there, indeed, more colloquial than an intelligent countenance, eagerly intent upon one while telling a story? What language can be compared to the speaking blush or flashing eye of an earnest listener? It was Desdemona, with greedy ear devouring his discourse, who won Othello's heart. He told his wondrous story, and she listened—that only was the witchcraft he had used."

It is said of Sir Walter Scott that, although one of the best talkers in the world, he was also the best listener. With the same bland look he would watch, throughout an entire evening, the lips of his garrulous tormentor ignorantly discoursing on Greek epigrams, or crassly dilating on the intricacies of a parliamentary debate.

It was said of Madame Récamier that she listened most winningly, and this was one secret of her wonderful power to charm.

We have all heard the story of Madame de Staël, who, by a clever stratagem, was introduced to a deaf mute at a party. She talked to him the whole evening, and afterward declared that never before had she met so intelligent a listener and so fine a conversationalist.

Do you remember the story told by Sterne in "The Sentimental Journey"?

He had been represented to a French lady as a great wit and an engaging converser, and the lady was impatient for an introduction that she might hear him talk.

They met, and, writes Sterne: "I had not taken my seat before I saw she did not care a sou whether I had any wit or no. I was to be convinced that she had. I call heaven to witness I never once opened the door of my lips."

The lady afterward said she never in her life had a more improving conversation with a man.

Many other instances might be mentioned derived from both fact and fiction, to show how attentive listening may enhance the delights of conversation, and that one may sometimes gain a reputation for conversational powers by exercising one's ear instead of one's tongue.

"A frequent caller at my home," said a lady, "is a capital story-teller, always instructive and pleasing; but she is a poor listener. When my part of the conversation comes in, her manner is depressing. I feel embarrassed, my words become tangled, my memory leaves me, and I hurry to close my remarks, conscious of having made a weak argument, although I had a point when I began.

My friend loses her easy manner when I speak, becomes restless, and breaks in upon me before I have fairly begun. Her unresponsive eyes tell me as plainly of her superiority as though she had written it in black and white."

Clergymen, teachers, and public speakers understand and appreciate better than others "the compliment of attention." Embarrassing, indeed, is it to anyone who is talking to observe signs of weariness and inattention on the part of one's hearers. Those not accustomed to stand before an audience seldom realize that a speaker feels and understands, without conscious endeavor, the attitude toward him of every member of his audience. The good listener inspires and encourages him, while the restless, inattentive auditor is a thorn in the flesh, irritating and distracting.

At the close of a lecture given a few years ago in a town in Maine, the lecturer—who was a state superintendent of schools—turned to the writer and asked:

"Who are those two ladies dressed in black, standing there by the window?"

After telling him their names the writer said, "Why do you ask?"

The lecturer replied: "They have been of great help to me all the evening. They are delightful listeners. They appeared to appreciate so thoroughly everything I said that I seemed to be talking especially for their benefit."

"That girl," said a teacher, pointing to an attractive young lady just leaving the school-room, "is the most restful pupil I ever had in my school. She is so gentle in her demeanor, so thoughtful and so attentive during recitations, that one cannot help loving her. No matter how restless the other members of the school become, she is always giving the closest attention. If one could have an entire school like her, teaching would be a delight; but she is one among fifty."

We gain many things besides the good will of others, by being good listeners, even though we must sometimes submit to be bored to an unlimited degree without interrupting the speaker, or responding in any other way than by "nods and becks and wreathéd smiles."

"Open your mouth and shut your eyes and see what heaven will send you," says the old maxim; but, "shut your mouth and open your eyes," has been suggested as much more sensible advice under some circumstances.

"But," you say, "we are told that Samuel Johnson, Tennyson and Macaulay, and many other great thinkers, usually monopolized the conversation when they were in company, and their friends delighted to listen to them. Surely they gave but little heed to 'the compliment of attention.'" Very true, but no doubt they would have been sometimes more agreeable to the company if they had been more considerate of the wishes of other people. Great men are great in spite of their weaknesses, not because of them. We can forgive unpleasant propensities in a genius more easily than in the average mortal, and as almost all of us are average mortals, without a trace of anything akin to genius, we cannot afford to dispense with any of those qualities which help to make us pleasing to others. We should remember that there was but one Macaulay—a man who could talk brilliantly on almost all subjects—and notwithstanding his brilliancy, his friends admitted that he was often something of a bore.

A very useful lesson may be learned from a little story which appeared some years ago in *The Youth's Companion*:

George Paul, a young civil engineer, while surveying a railway in the Pennsylvania hills, met a plain, lovable little country girl, and married her. After a few weeks he brought her home to his family in New York, and left her there while he returned to camp.

Marian had laid many plans to win the affections of her new kinsfolk. She had practiced diligently at her music; she was sure they would be pleased to hear her stories of her beautiful sister and her brother; she imagined their admiration of her new blue silk gown and winter bonnet. But the Pauls, one and all, were indifferent to her music, her family and her gowns. They gave "George's wife" a friendly welcome, and then each went on his or her way, and paid no more attention to her.

After the first shock of disappointment Marian summoned her courage.

"If I have nothing to give them, they have much to give me," she thought, cheerfully. She listened eagerly when Isabel sung, and her smiles and tears showed how keenly she appreciated the music. She examined Louisa's paintings every day with unflagging interest, discussed every effect, and was happy if she could help mix the colors or prepare the canvas. She questioned grandma about her neuralgia, advised new remedies, or listened unwearied to the account of old ones day after day. When Uncle John, just returned from Japan, began to describe his adventures, Marian was the only auditor who never grew tired nor interrupted him.

After a two hours' lecture, in which her part had been that of a dumb, bright-faced listener, Uncle John declared that George's wife was the most intelligent woman he had ever met.

When George came home the whole family was loud in her praises. She was a fine musician; she had unerring taste in art; she was charming, witty and lovable. But George soon saw that she had won them unconsciously—not by displaying her own merits, but by appreciating theirs.

This is a true story in fact, but the truth of its meaning is repeated wherever a woman is found who has that quality called charm. She may be plain or even deformed, but she will win friendship and love.

Many an attractive girl would save herself much anxiety and vain effort on her entrance into the world of society, if she understood that society, so called, is composed of individuals, the most of whom desire not to find the beauty, the wit, the talent of others, but to elicit the cordial recognition by others, of their own.

THE VOICE.

"Tender tones prevent severe truths from offending."

"There are tones which set commonplace words apart, and give them lights and deeps of meaning, just as one fine emotion idealizes and exalts a homely face."

"There is no power of love so effective as a kind voice. A kind hand is deaf and dumb. It may be rough in flesh and blood, yet do the work of a soft heart, and do it with a soft touch. But there is no one thing that love so much needs as a sweet voice to tell what it means and feels."

In our efforts to please, while much depends upon what we say, quite as much depends upon how we say it. The influence of a pleasing voice is wonderful; who has not felt its charm?

It has been said that the greatest defect in the American woman is her voice, and while this may not be strictly true, there are heard in conversation at home and abroad many voices more unpleasant than necessary—more harsh, more rasping.

A woman's voice may imply good breeding, or the reverse, and in estimating the power of feminine charms, a pleasing voice should be placed very near the head of the list. Is it not strange, then, that so little effort is made to remedy defects in vocal expression?

We cultivate the voice for singing and for elocutionary effects, but little is done for the average boy or girl by way of training the voice for the everyday effect. Only a few can sing well enough to give pleasure to others, but we all talk every day of our lives, and often the quality of our voice speaks more significantly than the words we utter. A sympathetic tone will often win us a friend, though what we say may be of little importance. Purity of accent plays a great part in the art of charming, and it has been truly said that "a woman may be ugly, old, without distinction or instruction, but if she have a soft, insinuating, mellow-toned voice, she will charm as much as her more beautiful sister."

A telephone operator in a place near New York was on a certain Christmas the recipient of checks for five, ten and a hundred dollars, a diamond pin, a dress pattern, and eight boxes of confectionery; although she was known to the donors only by her gentle voice, by the deference of its tone, by her readiness to accommodate, and by her office number as one of the operators.

Why is it that we regard vocal training and oral expression as something to be confined wholly to the specialists? We think such training is needed by public speakers and readers, and by all who intend to make a professional use of the voice, but we do not appreciate its value for the average man or woman.

"What should we think," says *Expression*, "of a woman who dresses in the richest of apparel, who is extremely careful of every point of dress, but who speaks with a nasal twang and throaty tone, and makes no effort to correct the fault? We know that this is often the case. Why is not the inconsistency corrected? Why is there no endeavor to improve the voice and make it beautiful and winning? What a sensitiveness people exhibit about going abroad with a smudge on the face; but, alas! there is little sensitiveness regarding a smudge on one's voice.

The truth is that voice culture should not be confined to the few, but should become a prescribed branch of the education of boys and girls generally. Not alone are the voices of the women too often unmelodious, but those of the men also need attention. A fine voice may be of inestimable value to a man. The majority of the celebrated orators have been aided by the possession of a good voice, along with the knowledge requisite to enable them to employ it effectively. Mr. Lecky says that O'Connell's voice, rising with a melodiously modulated swell, filled the largest auditoriums and triumphed over the wildest tumult, while at the same time it conveyed every shade of feeling with the most delicate flexibility.

Mr. Gladstone's voice is said to have had the musical quality and the resonance of a silver trumpet; while William Pitt, who was a ruler in Parliament at the age of twenty-one, possessed a voice of masterful power yet of a wonderful sweetness.

Webster's voice, on the occasion of his reply to Senator Dickinson, was so commanding, so forceful, that one of his listeners said he felt all the night as if a heavy cannonade had been resounding in his ears.

Garrick used to say that he would give one hundred guineas if he could say "Oh" as Whitefield would say it.

"But," you declare, "nature has not given us voices like the voices of those celebrated men, and we must be content with what we have."

While nature may not have bestowed upon us their melodious voices, we can do much to improve our own. A study of biography will inform us that many of the most successful speakers, whether actors or orators, have been men and women possessing some native defect of speech or figure which they resolutely mastered by patient, persevering application. We all know of Demosthenes' impediment of speech, and are familiar with the story of his months of struggle and his final success.

Savonarola, when he first spoke in the cathedral at Florence, was considered a failure, on account of his wretched voice and awkward manner. Phillips Brooks, one of the greatest preachers America has produced, was told by his college president that the ministry was out of the question for him because of his nervousness and the defects of his speech.

It would be easy to multiply instances to show that the most awkward body and the roughest voice may be brought under control. In fact, where the voice is imperfect and the man is obliged to make a determined effort to master it, he attains by this means, a mental vigor and an emotional strength and a flexibility of voice and mind, as well as a command over the body, which render his delivery in the highest degree effective.

Again, it is not sufficient that we have naturally a melodious voice; we must know how, or else learn how, to use it. There must be feeling and expression in one's tones. If we wish to express cordiality, words are futile unless the voice sounds the feeling we wish to express. We need to learn how to modulate the voice so as to make it a true reflex of the mind and mood. Unless it tells of sincerity, apologies fail to convince of a contrite spirit. Unless it conveys confidence, protestations are in vain; yet the very tone of one's voice may allay bitterness, though one may stumble over the words of an apology. If, then, one recognizes the fact that his voice is colorless and devoid of feeling, though his heart be warm, let him at once apply himself to remedying the defect.

Listen to your own voice when speaking, and note the harsh, strident tones, and the imperfect inflection, and correct them. Many girls speak in a nervous, jerky, rapid way, beginning a sentence and repeating a portion of it two or three times before completing it. Some speak in high, shrill tones which are not only displeasing but positively irritating because discordant. Some speak too fast, while others, going to the opposite extreme, simply drawl. These are defects which can be corrected, and, by correcting them we add measurably to our power to charm.

If you do not understand the imperfections of your tone productions, or the faults in your manner of speaking, or if you have trouble in correcting them, go to one who does know, and who is as sensitive to the speaking voice as he is to the singing voice. It may cost you something to do this, but it will be money judiciously expended. You take music lessons, both vocal and instrumental, and you do not consider the money expended for such lessons as wasted even though you have no intention of going upon the stage in opera or of becoming a professional pianist. You study music as an accomplishment. Why then should you not give some time, and if need be, a little money for the purpose of perfecting your speaking voice, if by so doing you can make yourself more agreeable to others. You may not be called upon very often to sing or play for other people, but you will talk every day and many times each day, and the voice is "the agent of the soul's expression."

"The art of singing," says *The Boston Herald,* "strange to say, does not include the art of speaking, for some very fine singers have harsh and unmusical voices in conversation. But with all the training now given to the rising generation, voice education should be considered. Take the rasp and the hardness out of your sons' and daughters' speech, and give them another grace with which to conquer society."

The importance of what we say and how we say it, has never been more clearly or pointedly expressed than in this quotation from an American writer: "A man may look like a monkey and yet turn out to be a philosopher; a man may dress like a vagabond, and yet have the intuitions of a scholar and a gentleman. The face, the expression of the eye, the dress, the manner even, may all be deceptive, but the voice and speech of men and women classify them infallibly."

GOOD MANNERS.

Life is not so short but that there is always time for courtesy.

Emerson.

"Politeness is real kindness kindly expressed. This is the sum and substance of all true politeness. Put it in practice and all will be charmed with your manner."

Young men generally would doubtless be thoroughly astonished if they could comprehend at a single glance how greatly their personal happiness, popularity, prosperity, and usefulness depend on their manners.

J. G. Holland.

In attracting others to us the value of a pleasing manner cannot be estimated. It is like sunshine. We feel it at once, and we are attracted to the person who possesses it.

"Give a boy address and accomplishments," said Emerson, "and you give him the mastery of palaces and fortunes wherever he goes; he has not the trouble of earning or owning them: they solicit him to enter and possess."

Much has been written upon this subject. Indeed, so much has been said, and said so well, that there will be little attempt to do anything else in this chapter than to bring together some of the best thoughts of the best authors.

The men and women who have accomplished great things in the world have, as a rule, understood the value of politeness, and have acted in accordance with that knowledge. You can, possibly, recall a very few exceptions, but these were persons great in spite of their lack of courtesy, and they would have been even greater had they practiced the art of gentle manners.

The Duke of Marlborough, whose general education was in some respects sadly neglected, had so irresistible a charm of manner that he swayed the destinies of nations. Mirabeau, who was unattractive in person, won by his politeness the good will of all with whom he came in contact. There has been no time in the history of the world when good manners counted for more than they do at the present time. In fact, to-day more than ever before a man is dependent for success upon his personality. Good manners often bring to one many things that wealth cannot procure, and "politeness has won more victories than powder."

"No one," says an American writer, "who has any appreciation of grace and beauty in nature or in art can fail to recognize the charm of fine manners in an individual. We rejoice in them as we do in a lovely sunset view, or a beautiful piece of architecture, or a fascinating poem, for their own sake and for what they express; but even beyond this they have another attraction in the magnetic power they exert upon all beholders in setting them at ease, in sweeping away shyness, awkwardness and restraint, and in stimulating them to the expression of whatever is best worth cherishing within them."

It is undoubtedly true that the presence of fine manners, whether it be in the home or the social circle, in the workshop or the counting-room, in the visit of charity or the halls of legislation, has an immediate effect in reproducing itself, in diffusing happiness, in developing the faculties, and in eliciting the best that is in everybody.

Surely there is no quality that a girl or a woman can possess which recommends her more favorably to the good opinion of others than that of uniform courtesy and good manners.

William Wirt's letter to his daughter on the "small, sweet courtesies of life," contains a passage from which a deal of happiness may be learned. "I want to tell you a secret. The way to make yourself pleasant to others is to show them attention. The whole world is like the miller at Mansfield, who cared for nobody—no not he, because nobody cared for him. And the whole world would serve you so, if you gave them the same cause. Let everyone, therefore, see that you do care for them by showing them the small courtesies in which there is no parade, whose voice is still to please; and which manifest themselves by tender and affectionate looks, and little acts of attention, giving others the preference in every little enjoyment at the table, walking, sitting, or standing."

Young men who wish to make their way in the world cannot afford to forget that there is not in all the world a talisman of such potent magic as the irresistible spell of a charming manner. While in some cases it seems innate, it can, in a great measure, be acquired. Yet a careful observer of the young men of the present generation cannot fail to notice a tendency, on the part of some at least, to disregard the small courtesies of life—the intangible, yet very perceptible little things which make the man a gentleman. Some people even contend that outward manner is a secondary consideration if the head is well stored with knowledge, and that if a young man has the faculty to get on in the world, it is a matter of very little importance if he have not the manners of a Chesterfield. That this idea is prevalent is accounted for by the great number of well-educated men—men of ability and power—who, clever and with no lack of brains, are painfully deficient in good breeding. With no intentional lapses they are awkward, presuming, and even vulgar.

"In most countries," says the *Toronto Week*, "an educated man and a gentleman are almost synonymous terms. On this side of the Atlantic they by no means always apply to the same man. Educational advantages are within the reach of all classes of people—even persons who have missed the benefit of home training for their manners, or who have not numbered cultured persons among their acquaintances. Such persons by native ability and hard work often attain to high positions of honor and trust in the various professions, and win for themselves the title of 'self-made.'

"Yet because a man by his brains, energy, and pluck carves out his own fortune, putting himself in a prominent position, is it not very desirable that he should also cultivate the courtesies of life so that the talent be not hidden by roughness and uncultivated bearing."

We frequently meet college students—especially from the smaller colleges—good, honest, earnest, ambitious fellows, who are working hard to make their way in the world. They are poor, and have come from homes where the stern realities of gaining a livelihood have left, apparently, no time for culture; where the table manners are but little better than those of the logging camp, and where the graces of refined speech and manners have never even taken root. They may take never so high a rank in their college studies, may pursue the work preparatory to a profession with never so much diligence, yet they will always be handicapped by their ignorance of those embellishments so necessary to social, and even business, success. They find themselves continually placed at a disadvantage, and their lack of social training is responsible for failures which might have been avoided.

Because a man is a successful lawyer he is not justified in saying that he can be his own tailor, or that ill-fitting clothes, if belonging to him and of his own make, are as suitable as those of a good cut. So it is with the intellectual giant who takes no heed of his manners. He may learn much from less talented persons, who are, nevertheless, his superiors in many respects. Desirable as it may be for a young man to shun the extravagance of the æsthete, and to despise the shams of society, he cannot afford to neglect the courtesies of life; and he does well who, while devoting his energies to mathematics and the classics, pays attention to the improvement of his manners. It is while young that manners are formed; the most strenuous efforts will not wholly eradicate in after life the awkward habits formed in youth.

The young man who is ambitious, upon whom Dame Fortune is already turning a dawning smile, should pause and think about this matter. Some time he may be rich; some time he may aspire to a high position in society or in public life, and he should begin early to fit himself for the proud position he means to occupy.

The outward address of a man has no little influence upon his success in business. The polite attention and readiness to meet every reasonable, and often unreasonable, demand of his customers, on the part of A. T. Stewart, when he opened his narrow linen store on Broadway, was almost as important a factor in his rapid success in securing business as his remarkable quickness in discovering changes in the market, and in adapting his goods to the taste and necessities of his patrons. This marked self-restraint and politeness of manner he retained to the last.

It is strange that every business man does not appreciate the commercial value of politeness. The writer knows a clerk who is employed in a drug store in one of the largest towns of Maine. So polite is he in his attentions to customers, so willing to be helpful, so pleasing in his manner, with that restraint and quietness which mark the gentleman and destroy every trace of effusion, that he has made himself invaluable to his employer. It is reported that, more than once, his friends have urged him to establish a business of his own, but his employer, realizing his value in attracting and holding customers, has turned him from the idea by a generous increase of salary. Thousands of clerks and thousands of professional and business men could greatly increase their earning power by closer attention to the accepted rules of courtesy.

Some people excuse a roughness of manner by saying that they detest affectations of all kinds, that they love the truth, that they are perfectly frank and outspoken. Such people pride themselves upon their naturalness, and on the ground of frankness they will wound by rude language, will insult you, and defend their awkwardness and ill-breeding by the plea of "natural manners." Naturalness is not always commendable. If nature has not invested us with those qualities which are pleasing to others, we should try to improve upon nature. The plainest truths may be conveyed in civil speech, and it is better to "assume a virtue if you have it not." To object to politeness on the ground that its language is sometimes unmeaning and expressed for effect, is as foolish as it would be to object to the decoration of our parlors or the wearing of good clothes.

In the ordinary compliments of good society there is no intention to deceive. Polite language is pleasant to the ear, and soothing to the heart, while rough words are the reverse, and while they may not always be the result of bad temper, they are quite likely to cause it.

The motive for politeness should not be the desire to shine, or to raise one's self into society supposed to be better than one's own. The cultivation of good manners is not merely a means to the gratification of personal vanity, but it is a duty we owe not only to other people but to ourselves; a duty to make ourselves better in every respect than we are. Indeed, the true spirit of good manners is so nearly allied to that of good morals that they seem almost inseparable.

"Did you ever think how invisible is the armor of defence afforded by perfect politeness?" asks *Harper's Bazar*. "Neither man, woman nor child can resist it. The quick tempered Irish maid who loses her hold on her tongue so easily and 'answers back' with a hot retort is abashed when her mistress meets her with quiet courtesy. The angry person, off guard and saying what he really does not mean, is foiled by the self-control of his interlocutor, who has not, for an instant, forgotten the gracious manner of good breeding."

Politeness is, perhaps, instinctive with some, but with the majority it is a matter of training, of the slow and careful discipline of voice and eye and carriage. Under this training all the angles of personal vanity and self-consciousness are rubbed off, the person becomes adorned with grace, ease, simplicity and gentleness, and what may seem to the untrained observer as the perfection of naturalness may be simply the perfection of culture.

Very sensitive persons who suffer acutely from fancied slights can save themselves many wounds by always being as scrupulous in giving as they are in exacting courtesy. To suffer one's self to perpetrate a rudeness is to lay one's self open to the same. In nothing should we be less economical than in politeness. It should lead us to prompt and generous acknowledgment of every kindness, to responsive thanks when a gift, however small, is brought to our door. It should oblige us to listen with patient attention even to the person whose conversation is not entertaining, to sit apparently absorbed when in public we are present at concert or lecture. This defensive armor, so smooth, so polished, so easily worn, will make our intercourse with society agreeable.

The fact is, that when we come in contact with human beings anywhere and in any occupation, we are quite likely to get in return just what we give.

A man who is always the gentleman seldom meets with rebuffs from even the most unpolished and crude. The employer who uses kind words with his workmen, usually gets kind words in return.

DRESS.

"No woman is ugly who is well dressed."

Spanish Proverb.

For the apparel oft proclaims the man.

Hamlet.

I believe in dress. I believe that God delights in beautiful things, and as he has never made anything more beautiful than woman, I believe that that mode of dressing the form and face which best harmonizes with her beauty is that which pleases him best.

J. G. Holland.

As the author of this volume is a man, this chapter on dress is, of course, written from a man's point of view. He knows very well that, were he to attempt to write scientifically of woman's clothes he would be lost. No one but a woman can do that. The man who tried it would soon find himself bewildered by a maze of technical terms and expressions which seem absolutely necessary to describe exactly what is meant. Possibly, however, the author can take a broad, mental grasp of the subject apart from and above the pretty finesse with which feminine writers would treat the subject. Clothes are the woman's weapons, one of the resources of civilization, with which woman marches forth to the conquest of the masculine world, and the writer wishes to estimate from the man's standpoint just how much the silks, the laces, the ribbons and the velvets have to do in influencing the masculine heart.

What one wears is accepted as an index of one's character. Whether this is as it should be or not, yet it is true; and we all feel, more or less, that coarseness or refinement finds visible expression in apparel as in no other way. "Surely," says *The Boston Journal,* "nothing so intensifies the personality as the clothes one wears; through association they become a part of us, help to identify us, even in some peculiar, reactionary way, serve to control our mental states."

Many women will tell you that their most infallible cure for weariness and the blues is to go and dress up in one of their prettiest gowns. Many men will tell you that a clean shave, clean linen, and a fresh suit of clothes are most reviving and soothing in their effect upon the psychical as well as the physical man.

The statement, often made, that women dress well only to please the men, is only a fraction of the truth.

They dress to please the men; to please one another, and to please themselves. Which of these three motives is the strongest depends upon the individual, for,—"while there are men and men, there are women and women and women," and it is absurd to make any attempt to analyze motives or to formulate principles which will apply to all women.

The men who dress well do it for the women and for themselves. The effect that their apparel has upon others of their own sex, gives men but little concern. If all the women should be taken from the world tailors would at once lose half their business, for the men would immediately begin to wear out their old clothes.

As a rule, few men care very much for fine clothes for their own sake, but a love of dress is natural in woman, and one who exhibits indifference in regard to her personal appearance convicts herself of either indolence, self-righteousness or pedantry. A woman who has not some natural taste in dress, who does not take a positive delight in combinations of colors, who is not fond of fine apparel for its own sake, is an anomaly.

Men do not notice details of a woman's dress. Few know enough about the subject to distinguish cheese-cloth from *point d'esprit*. The description in detail of a new gown as given in a fashion journal is about as intelligible to the average man as the inscriptions on an Assyrian tablet.

They accept the woman as a whole, and consider her, and what she has on, as one harmonious, homogeneous, unanalyzable completeness. If you doubt this ask a man to tell you how a certain lady was dressed at a reception he attended the evening before. Perhaps he noticed her particularly while there, and told you at the time that she was becomingly attired. He may be able to tell you that she wore a pink waist, or that the prevailing color of her costume was blue, but there his knowledge of the subject ends.

While it is true that men give but little thought to the details of a woman's dress, unless it is conspicuously bad, very many of them know whether she is becomingly attired or not. While they may have no clear idea as to whether the material of a gown cost five cents or five dollars a yard, or whether the gown itself is quite in fashion, they know whether the owner carries it well, and whether the material, style and color are becoming to her. Perhaps, on the whole, a man of good taste is a better judge than a woman as to whether she is becomingly dressed. This is because they regard the subject from entirely different stand points. The stylishly gowned woman is, to the average woman, well dressed, but not necessarily so to the man. It is a perpetual wonder to some men why women have not the courage to reject certain combinations and certain styles of dress that are inharmonious and ugly in themselves, and, consequently, unbecoming to the one who wears them.

Years ago certain colors were thought to be becoming to certain types of women. There was an undisputed tradition in regard to the colors which the blonde should wear, and also what ones were becoming to the brunette. This was not a dictate of fashion; it was a fact ascertained by experience. Of late these traditions have been disregarded by fashion, and the stylish woman wears any color or combination she pleases, but often at the sacrifice of her good looks.

Fashion cannot change the laws of cause and effect—the laws of harmony—and if the decided brunette chooses to wear colors which are becoming only to blondes she does it at the expense of half her natural beauty. Men feel this and wonder what is amiss.

A few years ago fashion made quite common a style of sailor hat with diminutive crown made in the shape of an hour-glass. They were ugly in themselves, and when perched upon the head detracted from the beauty of any face. Nothing could be more ridiculous than the sight of a stout, tall girl, with broad hips and prominent features, marching along the street with her head surmounted by that parody on the most becoming of all hats for a young woman—the sailor. One at once called to mind the dice-box which the negro minstrel wears to make himself appear as funny as possible. One man wittily characterized them as "the hats that wore corsets." Men never liked them, but thousands of them were worn.

From a man's point of view it would be far better if women made a more comprehensive and sensible study of their individual needs in dress and did not blindly follow the decrees of fashion; if more women would realize that the garment suitable to a tall, slim figure, is utterly inappropriate to a stout, short one. When Sara Bernhardt invented the glove which was to give size and form to her thin and poorly shaped arm, she recognized the highest aim of fashion. When a woman is in need of a new hat or bonnet, a man's advice would be: "Hunt the tables until you find one which, in shape and trimming, is suitable and becoming to you. Never mind if it is not the very latest style; if it suits your face and figure, take it, and you will not be sorry."

In furnishing a room we understand that we should put in it only what makes the room look better—not what is simply pretty in itself; and if women would follow a similar plan in dress,—wear only what is becoming to them, and not wear things, simply because they think them pretty and fashionable, men would be better pleased. Man is attracted by a woman's beauty itself, and whether she has just the latest modes or not seldom interests him in the least. So the girl who would dress to please men, should, first of all, wear what will show off her natural attractiveness of face and figure to the best advantage; after that she may be as fashionable as possible.

Without doubt many girls attach too much importance to dress as a means of attracting the other sex. It is frequently the case that, when a young lady is invited to a social function, her first thought is, "What shall I wear?" Her second thought is, "What shall I wear?" This question is with her much of the time until she goes to the place where she is to be entertained; and as she enters the room her first thought is, "I wonder how I look." If, upon an examination of the other young ladies present, she concludes that she is as well dressed as anyone there, she experiences a feeling of restfulness and of satisfaction, and enjoys the evening. She imagines she must be an object of interest to the men, and to an extent she is.

Men like women to be "well groomed." They take in her whole appearance at a glance, and then pay but little further attention to the question of gowns, ribbons, slippers or sashes. They want to be entertained and amused. If the only preparation a young lady has made to render herself attractive and interesting is the care bestowed upon her personal appearance; if her resources for attracting consist only of a pretty face and a graceful figure in a pretty gown, she will never become famous for her conquests.

Simplicity and exquisitely fresh neatness and daintiness are to a man more attractive than any extravagance of fashion or costliness of material. No man was ever induced to propose to a girl by the splendor of her costume. Of course it would be absurd to assert that physical beauty is of no value, or that dress is of little importance. That girl who is born physically beautiful, is fortunate indeed, and any girl of common sense knows that an attractive gown or a becoming hat is of importance. The great thing for her to understand is that there must be something better under the becoming hat than a pretty face, for her own happiness, and if she would be very attractive to others.

Just as there are some persons who are said to be born magnetic, so some women are supposed to have a peculiarly attractive way of wearing clothes which defies imitation.

Said a writer in the *Springfield Republican*: "There is a subtle something which one cannot get on the microscopic slide, which refuses to be reduced to percentages, which baffles description, and that is the manner in which some women wear their clothes. Two girls with faces of equal value and garments of identical texture will fail to produce equivalent effects, because one has this indefinable quality, and the other has not. Consequently we often hear it said that some girls are more attractive in calico than others in richer material."

That there is a marked difference in the way different women wear their clothes, no one will deny, but because some girls look and appear to better advantage than others in the same material, is it necessary to regard it as beyond comprehension, or to declare that it "baffles description"? The writer did not go far enough in his description of the two girls. While their faces were of equal value, and their clothing was of the same material, there might be other differences which would account for the "indefinable quality." Possibly one was pleasing in manner and the other not. One was awkward in person and in speech, while the other was tactful and graceful. One was dull; the other interesting. The difference was one of physical and mental characteristics, and not a quality that "baffles description." Indeed it is a difference easily understood and analyzed.

If two girls have faces and forms of equal value, and are equally graceful, tactful and well mannered, their clothes, if of the same form and material, will be worn in much the same way, and will produce much the same effect.

No man, whatever his position in the world may be, can afford to be careless about his personal appearance. Dress may not make the man, but we all form in our minds a very clear idea of what a man is by his dress. We gain our first impression of persons by what they have on; our second judgment is formed from their conversation and manner.

The well dressed man is more attractive to others, and he feels much better himself than he would if carelessly attired. Have you noticed the wonderful transformation which takes place in a man when he doffs his everyday clothes and dons a dress suit? During the day he may have an untidy and even a slovenly appearance, but as soon as he puts on a well laundered shirt, a high standing collar, a fresh lawn tie, and a dress suit, he seems completely changed. He looks from five to ten years younger, and from his manner you know that he feels younger. He is on better terms with himself and with the world.

Every woman likes a man better for being well dressed. She may excuse, or overlook, carelessness or even slovenliness in his personal appearance, if she is very fond of him, but she would like him much more if he were neat and tidy and tasteful. She may forgive his green and yellow necktie, she may overlook his soiled linen, she may make no reference to his coat with its collar covered with dust and dandruff; she may not let him know that she has even noticed any of these things, but she has. She thinks of them whenever he is with her, and sometimes when she is away from him, and she wishes he were different. She may like him in spite of these defects. Women usually like a man in spite of things. If a man noticed half as many things about a woman that did not please him, he would never love her at all.

Leaving out of the question the fact that women like to have men neat and even elegant in their raiment, no man who is seeking to make his way in business or in a profession, can afford to be careless about his clothes.

"A few men," says *The Lewiston Journal,* "clothed in the serenity of soul that approaches the insanity of genius can afford to go illy-clothed. President Lincoln was given free license to wear frock coats unbecomingly. Horace Greeley could wear a linen duster with grace and equanimity. But they were unique. They could make fashion look insignificant, but you and I cannot, if we care to move amid the throng of busy people seeking passage on the car of progress."

No better advice has been given to men on the subject of dress than in an article which appeared in *Success.* A short extract from the article will close this chapter.

"Clothes are one of the accepted standards by which men are judged the world over. They form the chief standard of first impression; so, for that reason alone, it would be difficult to overestimate their importance. They show at a glance whether a man is neat or untidy; careful or careless; methodical or shiftless, and what sort of taste he has. Nothing else about him reflects so much of his personal characteristics. So it is not surprising to be told by those who yearly give employment to thousands of men and boys, that more applicants are turned away on account of their personal appearance than for all other reasons put together. But it would surprise some people very much if they knew how widely this rule is applied.

The well dressed man is one whose clothes do not make him the object of comment, either because they are showy or shabby. He never goes to the extremes of fashion, thereby courting notoriety; he never goes to the other extreme by paying no attention at all to what he wears or how he wears it. He is always modest in his attire. He conforms to the established customs of changing his attire as the occasion demands, without making himself a slave to reform. He does not always wear expensive clothes, nor is it at all necessary that he should. But he is always clean and neat, or, as the present day has it, he is "well groomed."

THE OPTIMIST.

The habit of looking on the bright side of things is worth far more than a thousand pounds a year.

—Samuel Johnson.

"More than half the unhappiness in the world comes from a person's unwillingness to look on the bright side so long as a dark side can be discovered."

We all like the optimist. The bright, cheerful, good-natured fellow, who always looks through the cloud and sees its silver lining, is as good as a tonic to our most pessimistic dispositions. If, then, you wish to make yourself agreeable to others and to yourself, cultivate the habit of cheerfulness—of always looking on the bright side. Wear a pleasant countenance; let cheerfulness beam in your eye; let love write its mark on your forehead, and have kind words and a pleasant greeting for those whom you meet. Don't forget to say "good morning!" and say it heartily. Say it to your brothers and sisters, your school-mates, your parents, your teachers and your friends. Pleasant, hearty greetings cheer the discouraged, rest the tired, and make the wheels of life run more smoothly. They clear up the thorny pathways, win friends, and confound enemies. In fact, it is impossible to resist the influence of cheerfulness. Let a bright face beam on the darkness of defeat, shine on the abode of poverty; illumine the chamber of sickness, and how everything changes under its benign influence.

Victory becomes possible, competence promises a golden future, and health is wooed back again.

On the other hand, you cannot estimate the amount of unhappiness you may cause by wearing a clouded face and by speaking harsh, unkind words.

Many persons fret and whine all through life. They never appear to have a generous impulse.

"They seem to have come into the world during one of those cold, bleak, gloomy days, when there was nothing with which to build a fire. They, apparently, grew up in the same bleak atmosphere, and they live in it all their lives. You see their smallness in everything they do and say. You see it in their buying and in their selling, in their talk and in their actions. They have been well called 'the frogs that constitute one of the plagues of society.' They have never made one heart glad, nor shed one ray of sunshine upon man, woman, or child."

It is just as easy to be kind as to be cross, and as easy to give pleasure as pain. It costs nothing; it is a smile, an appreciative word, a mention of what one likes to hear spoken of rather than an irritating reference.

If your minister has preached a sermon that interested and helped you, tell him so. It will encourage and cheer him, and he will try to give you still better sermons in the future. Remember that the preacher is much more human than most people think, and that no man more highly prizes the genuine, manly word of good cheer, sympathy and affection. If your grocer has sold you something that was particularly good, tell him so. No doubt you have often found fault with the tea and the flour and the meat; then why not surprise him by letting him know that you appreciate a good thing when you get it.

Perhaps you have children who are attending the public schools. Perhaps their teacher by patience, tact, and the expenditure of much nerve force, has succeeded in interesting them in their studies as they have never been before. Don't you think it would stimulate her to still greater effort if you should say to her when you meet: "My children are doing well at school this term. They like you and are interested in their work." No doubt you have often severely criticised teachers, methods, and school management, and you have been very free with your words of condemnation. Why not help a little by some expression of approval if you can honestly do so.

Give pleasure to your wife, if you have one. Notice her painstaking efforts to make home comfortable; compliment her dinner and show that you appreciate the thousand things she does for your comfort. There is no greater exhibition of heroic fortitude than is seen in one who dwells in a cheerless home she does her best to brighten, and who wears away the years in an unsatisfied desire for words and tokens of love and sympathy which never come to her.

Do not be afraid of giving something of yourself, of letting yourself out a little; and do not fear that your heart will run away with your head. Do not confound sentiment with sentimentalism, and do not hesitate to praise a thing or an act if it is really worthy of it. You need to do this for your own sake as well as for the sake of making others happy.

"For my own sake," you say. "In what way will it help me if I bestow praise upon another?" Praise, when it is deserved, is of more importance to the giver than the receiver.

"Praise does not immediately affect the merit of him to whom it is awarded," said a writer recently, "but it does immediately affect the merit of him to whom its awarding belongs. If a man deserves praise he is quite as much of a man without it as with it; but no man can be so much of a man, nor seem so much of a man, while withholding just praise as while bestowing it."

In little matters as well as in large ones, to acknowledge the merit of others is a duty, the performance of which is even more important to the one who owes it, than to the one to whom it is owed. We do not fail to express our appreciation of heroic deeds, but it is in the common, everyday life that the words of appreciation are most sorely needed, and too seldom spoken. Many a woman would have been greatly cheered and helped over many hard places, if, while living, she could have heard half as many nice things said to her by those she loved, as were put into her funeral sermon and obituary notice.

There is, of course, a great difference between the expression of a due and delicate appreciation of merit, and that false and exaggerated praise which is dictated by the desire to flatter. The former is always received with pleasure, but the latter wounds the susceptibility of those on whom it is lavished. To a mind rightly constituted, there are few things more painful than undeserved, or even excessive commendation. Flattery is never excusable; deserved praise should never be withheld.

Do not be a grumbler. Is there any person more unwelcome than the chronic growler? When we meet him he begins by growling about the weather; then you are entertained with a long account of his aches and pains, his trials and his losses. Nothing pleases him. His neighbors are dishonest, church members are hypocrites, public officials are, in his estimation, all rascals, law makers are corrupt, and the country is going to the dogs. If you speak in commendation of an individual, he at once attempts to belittle him in your estimation. If you praise a cause or an institution, he is sure to find fault with what you say. He wishes your sympathy for his troubles, but he has none to give.

We all crave sympathy, but, if we are not careful, we may exhaust the patience, even of our best friends, with the recital of our troubles. If your aches and pains are ever so bad, the best advice for you is "grin and bear it." It is all very well to be an interesting invalid for a short time. Your neighbors will bring you in good things to eat, and your friends will bring you pretty flowers to look at, and books to read, but do not remain too long in bed if you can help it, and do not wear too long and sad a face when you are recovering. It will not relieve your pain at all to tell everyone you meet how much you suffer, and when your friends have sympathized with you a dozen times they become a little tired of it. This advice is worthy of practice, not for the sake of your friends only, but for your own. The burden cheerfully borne becomes light, and any physician knows that the hopeful, cheerful patient has many more chances of recovery than the despondent one. In the lives of us all there are hours of anxiety, disappointment, pain and vexation; seasons of trial that are to be met only with stubborn patience. Greatness of soul is tested by the serenity with which these inevitable ills are borne and finally overcome. The little mind will fret and chafe and fume over little things, even as the petty stream over its narrow, pebbly bed, while the deep, strong river moves swiftly and silently over the boulders that lie at its bottom.

"But," you say, "while the advice is good it is very hard to follow it." Yes, but it is really harder not to heed it. "The bird that beats against the iron bars of its cage suffers more than the patient captive."

Laugh all you can. It is good for you. Physicians tell us that laughing has a direct and positive effect upon one's health. The physical movement caused by a hearty laugh causes the arteries to dilate and the flow of blood to hasten, thus promoting an acceleration of vital processes; and a mental action through stimulating the blood vessels of the brain. He who administers medicine in the shape of wit and humor to the sad heart is most assuredly a "good Samaritan."

The irresistible, good-humored philosophy of Mark Twain has relieved the depression and sorrow of multitudes. He has compelled us to laugh, and his mission in the world has been a beneficent one. A cheerful face is as good for an invalid as pleasant weather. Cheerfulness is health, melancholy is disease. Cheerfulness is just as natural to the heart of a man in sound moral and physical health as color to his cheeks, and wherever we see habitual gloom we may be sure there is something radically wrong in the animal economy or the moral sense.

Sydney Smith once gave a lady two-and-twenty receipts against melancholy. One was a bright fire; another, to remember all the pleasant things said to her; another, to keep a box of sugar plums on the chimney piece and a kettle simmering on the hob. These are trivial things in themselves but life is made up of these little pleasures and none should be neglected because of their seemingly trifling nature.

If our temperament does not make us naturally cheerful, we can, at least, cultivate those habits of body and mind which seem most favorable to the growth of this condition. We can keep the mind open to cheerful impressions, and close it to those that are gloomy. It is far better to magnify our blessings than to depreciate them. The Spaniard of whom Southey tells that he always put on his magnifying glasses when he ate cherries, in order to make them seem larger, had the true philosophy of life. So the ancient Pompeiians seem to have well understood the art of making the most of everything. Their gardens were very small, but by painting the surrounding walls with plants and landscapes their little area became indefinitely enlarged to the eye of the observer.

PERSONAL PECULIARITIES.

"Eccentricity may be harmless, but it never can be commendable; it is one of the children of that prolific failing—vanity. And whether it shows in feeling, manners, or peculiarities of dress, it is clearly acted upon from the presumptuous supposition that the many are in the wrong, the individual in the right."

Society will pardon much to genius and special gifts, but, being in its nature a convention, it loves what is conventional or what belongs to coming together. That makes the good and bad of manners, namely, what helps or hinders fellowship.

Emerson.

We all know that the outward address of a person has great influence upon his success both in the social and the business world. Thousands of men and women are, in their efforts to please, hindered by some personal peculiarity which is painfully apparent to other people, but of which they themselves seem wholly ignorant. Thousands of professional and business men are prevented from attaining the success they might reach by some infelicity of manner or speech which could be remedied by a little painstaking effort.

Here is a physician who has prepared himself thoroughly for his profession by years of hard study and by the expenditure of a considerable sum of money, but he knows little of human nature, and but little of the requirements of good society. He has no tact, and has not thought it necessary to cultivate that quality. He is cold and unsympathetic. He has no ability to make friends or to keep them. He is not sociable, and he does not make himself agreeable to his patients by those little kindly acts and sympathetic speeches so comforting to invalids. He feels that he is well prepared to practice his profession, and he regards any personal defects as of little importance. Other men of less ability, but with more tact, soon outstrip him in the race for public favor. He never succeeds in acquiring a large practice, and, possibly, never knows the reason why.

A young man applies for a position as a teacher. He is well equipped in scholarship for the place he wishes, for he led his class in college, and he comes highly recommended as a young man of integrity and earnestness. After a short interview the superintendent of schools decides that he is not the man for the position and the applicant goes away disappointed. Why was he rejected? Not by reason of poor scholarship, nor for lack of moral character, but simply on account of his personal appearance. He was untidy in his dress. His linen was soiled, his coat was not brushed, his cuffs were frayed at the edges, while his finger-nails gave evidence that he was habitually careless about personal neatness and cleanliness. The superintendent decided at once that he did not want him, and the young man did not know why.

Here is a young woman who is fine looking, intelligent and accomplished. Apparently she possesses all those qualities which are necessary to make her a favorite in society and she seems to deserve a host of friends. Yet she is not greatly sought after by her acquaintances, and she has few firm friends. Young men pay her but little attention, and seem afraid of her. Other girls, less brilliant intellectually, with fewer accomplishments, and with plainer faces, are far greater favorites in society. Her particular weakness is that she has allowed herself to fall into the practice of employing sarcasm to an extent which is offensive to those with whom she talks. She has a habit of saying disagreeable, biting things in a humorous way, and she never suspects that people are hurt by them. She has cultivated the habit to such a degree that she can always raise a laugh at some person's expense, and she is constantly on the watch for opportunities to exercise this accomplishment. Finally it dawns upon her that she does not hold her friends; that she is sometimes slighted in the matter of invitations; that she is not a popular girl, and she doesn't know why.

A certain clergyman is a fine preacher, capable of attracting, instructing, and inspiring the most cultivated audiences, but he is shut out from his proper sphere of usefulness and influence, and prevented from reaching the position for which his endowments qualify him, by a matter which might seem trifling in itself, but which has become offensive through its persistent hold upon him. He exhibits a lack of proper deference to the feelings of others, an arrogant and unsympathetic tone of voice, and sometimes yields, under opposition, to unrestrained violence of language. He betrays his weakness every time anyone crosses his plans and desires. It seems hard for him to understand that others have an equal right to their preference and opinions. He forgets that while it is easy to be amiable when everyone agrees with him, the test of character is in keeping the temper sweet and reasonable when people differ from him and criticise him. He understands his power to move audiences; he is told by persons competent to judge that his sermons are superior; he knows that in higher intellectual qualities he surpasses many other clergymen who secure and retain prominent positions; yet the painful truth is forced upon him that his services as a pastor are not sought for, while inferior preachers are selected for places of power and influence.

A man goes into trade. He is a shrewd buyer, energetic, honest, and keeps a good assortment of goods, but he is not obliging to customers. He is short and crusty in his speech, irritable and sometimes almost rude in his manner; consequently he does not hold his patrons. They leave him, one by one, and do their purchasing at other stores where they receive polite attention. The merchant does not prosper in business, and he never knows why.

Here is a woman who prides herself upon her plain speaking. She boasts that when she has anything to say she is willing to say it to one's face, and not behind one's back. She thinks it is a mark of sincerity and frankness to say disagreeable things and to bring one's infirmities to the surface. Her tendencies finally become fixed habits. She finds herself shunned by her acquaintances, and she does not know why.

Then there is the loquacious woman, the woman who monopolizes the conversation, the woman who has an apparent contempt for paragraph and punctuation. No matter what the topic of conversation may be, she at once takes the management of it into her own hands, and the other members of the company are made to feel at once that they are expected to be only listeners. The loquacious woman may talk well—she often does—but she fails to understand that there may be such a thing as too much even of good things, and so she talks on and on, with an utter disregard for the rights and the comfort of those around her.

A professional man, who possesses much intellectual force and originality, takes pride in his unconventionality in the matter of dress. His garments are so far from the prevailing style that they attract attention and invite comment. He does not realize that the man who rebels against fashion may be open even more to the imputation of vanity than he who obeys it, because he makes himself conspicuous, and practically announces that he is wiser than his associates. An affectation of superior simplicity is vulgarity.

Stop a moment and recall twenty men and women of your acquaintance. You will probably remember that two-thirds of them have some peculiarity, some defect of speech or manner which detracts from their social and business success, or from their usefulness. One is a gossip; another possesses a hasty temper, while a third is intellectually dishonest, never yielding his position, even under the most absolute proof that he is in the wrong. One of your friends is a pessimist, and is continually attempting to convert you to his point of view, while his wife is so inquisitive that you at once become nervous when you perceive her approach. A young woman of your acquaintance would be a most charming person if she did not laugh too much. A conversation with her is, upon her part, a perpetual giggle.

These may generally be good, intelligent, and, in many respects, charming people, but unfortunately they are hampered by these deficiencies. They have become so unconscious of these personal traits that, doubtless, they would be greatly surprised were their attention called to them. The effect of these shortcomings upon others is, however, just as unfortunate as if they were intentionally retained and nourished, for we usually regard the outward manner as a true index of the inward emotion.If so many of our acquaintances display idiosyncrasies that affect us disagreeably, is it not possible that we too may be harboring some remediable evil of temper, some superable infirmity of manner or of speech which is a bar to our own usefulness, because distressing to those with whom we are thrown?

Let us think about this.

SUGGESTIONS FROM MANY SOURCES

FOR

THE MAN WHO WOULD PLEASE AND THE WOMAN WHO WOULD CHARM.

A gentleman makes no noise; a lady is serene.

Emerson.

So I talked a great deal and found myself infinitely pleased with Brandon's conversational powers, which were rare; being no less than the capacity for saying nothing, and listening politely to an indefinite deal of the same thing, in another form, from me.

Charles Major.

Talk about those subjects you have had long in your mind, and listen to what others say about subjects you have studied but recently. Knowledge and timber should not be much used till they are seasoned.

O. W. Holmes.

A beautiful form is better than a beautiful face; a beautiful behavior is better than a beautiful form; it gives a higher pleasure than statues or pictures; it is the finest of the fine arts.

Emerson.

Believe nothing against another but on good authority, nor report what may hurt another, unless it be a greater hurt to another to conceal it.

William Penn.

"Life is like a mirror. It reflects the face you bring to it. Look out lovingly upon the world, and the world will look lovingly in upon you."

But it is mostly my own dreams I talk of, and that will somewhat excuse me for talking of dreams at all. Everyone knows how delightful the dreams are that one dreams one's self, and how insipid the dreams of others are. I had an illustration of this fact not many evenings ago, when a company of us got telling dreams. I had by far the best dreams of any; to be quite frank, mine were the only dreams worth listening to; they were richly imaginative, delicately fantastic, exquisitely whimsical, and humorous in the last degree; and I wondered that when the rest could have listened to them they were always eager to cut in with some silly, senseless, tasteless thing, that made me sorry and ashamed for them. I shall not be going too far if I say that it was on their part the grossest betrayal of vanity that I ever witnessed.

William Dean Howells.

"There is a great mistake in supposing that giving is concerned only with material benefits. These form indeed but a small part of its mission. Whoever creates happiness, whether by a kindly greeting, or tender sympathy, or inspiring presence, or stimulating thought, is as true a giver as he who empties his purse to feed the hungry."

Politeness and good breeding are absolutely necessary to adorn any or all other good qualities or talents. Without them no knowledge, no perfection whatever, is seen in its best light. The scholar, without good breeding, is a pedant; the philosopher, a cynic; the soldier a brute; and every man, disagreeable.

Lord Chesterfield.

"Tact, though partly a natural gift, is a good deal indebted to education and early habits. The superiority of one sex to the other in this respect will often be found to depend on art quite as much as upon nature."

"Never is silence more eloquent than when it is preserved toward persons older than ourselves when they voice opinions long since proven erroneous. Age doesn't like to be contradicted, right or wrong."

In the supremacy of self-control consists one of the perfections of the ideal man: not to be impulsive, not to be spurred hither and thither by each desire that in turn comes uppermost; but to be restrained, self-balanced, governed by the joint decision of the feelings in council assembled, before whom every action shall have been fully debated and calmly determined.

Herbert Spencer.

In the exhaustless catalogue of heaven's mercies to mankind, the power we have of finding some germs of comfort in the hardest trials must ever occupy the foremost place; not only because it supports and upholds us when we most require to be sustained, but because in this source of consolation there is something, we have every reason to believe, of the Divine Spirit; something which, even in our fallen nature we possess in common with the angels.

Dickens.

"When you bury animosity don't set up a headstone over its grave."

I don't never hav truble in regulating mi own kondukt, but tew keep other pholks straight iz what bothers me.

Josh Billings.

"Hundreds of the most agreeable persons in fashionable society are those who are content to be taught the things they already know."

It is better to return a dropped fan genteelly than give a thousand pounds awkwardly; you had better refuse a favor gracefully than grant it clumsily. All your Greek can never advance you from secretary to envoy, or from envoy to embassador, but your address, your air, your manner, if good, may.

Lord Chesterfield.

"The art of not hearing should be learned by all. It is fully as important to domestic happiness as a cultivated ear, for which both money and time are expended. There are so many things which it is painful to hear, so many which we ought not to hear, so very many which if heard will disturb the temper, corrupt simplicity and modesty, detract from contentment and happiness that everyone should be educated to take in or shut out sounds according to his or her pleasure."

Once A Week.

"The bitterest tears shed over graves are for words left unsaid and deeds left undone. She never knew how I loved her. He never knew what he was to me. I always meant to make more of your friendship. I did not know what he was to me till he was gone. Such are the poisoned arrows which cruel death shoots back at us from the door of the sepulchre."

We are only really alive when we enjoy the good will of others.

Goethe.

A difference of taste in jokes is a great strain on the affections.

George Eliot.

"Power hath not one-half the might of gentleness."

Manner is of importance. A kind no is often more agreeable than a rough yes.

Bengel.

We are always clever with those who imagine we think as they do. To be shallow you must differ from people; to be profound you must agree with them.

Bulwer.

If you want to spoil all that God gives you; if you want to be miserable yourself and a maker of misery to others, the way is easy enough. Only be selfish, and it is done at once.

Charles Kingsley.

Language was given us that we might say pleasant things.

Bovee.

"The specially social qualities are good nature, amiability, the desire to please, and the kindness of heart that avoids giving offence. A good natured person may frankly disagree with you, but he never offends."

Good manners are made up of petty sacrifices.

Emerson.

Pride of origin, whether high or low, springs from the same principle of human nature; one is but the positive, the other the negative pole of a single weakness.

Lowell.

The best possible impression that you can make by your dress is to make no separate impression at all; but so to harmonize its material and shape with your personality, that it becomes tributary in the general effect, and so exclusively tributary that people cannot tell after seeing you what kind of clothes you wear.

J. G. Holland.

Nothing is more dangerous than to paint men as they are when by chance they are not as handsome as they would wish to be.

Edmond About.

"Borrow trouble if you have not enough already."

Refinement creates beauty everywhere.

Hazlitt.

"A lady may always judge of the estimation in which she is held by the conversation which is addressed to her."

Some people cannot drive to happiness with four horses, and others can reach the goal on foot.

Thackeray.

"The clown who excites the multitudes to mirth is more a benefactor than the conqueror who drapes a thousand homes in mourning."

"Tact is the art of putting yourself in another's place, and being quick about it."

"It pays 100 per cent. to be polite to everyone, from the garbage gatherer to the governor."

"If you wish that your own merit should be recognized, recognize the merits of others."

"If you cannot be happy in one way, be happy in another; and this facility of disposition wants but little aid from philosophy, for health and good humor are almost the whole affair. Many run about after felicity, like an absent man hunting for his hat while it is on his head or in his hand. Such persons want nothing to make them the happiest people in the world but the knowledge that they are so."

"An Atchison woman, who three days ago was considered the most popular woman in town, has not one friend left; instead of sympathizing with her friends, as she has heretofore, she began telling them her troubles."

Atchison Globe.

It is the characteristic of folly to discern the faults of others and to forget one's own.

Cicero.

What is it to be a gentleman? It is to be honest, to be gentle, to be generous, to be brave, to be wise, and, possessing all these qualities, to exercise them in the most graceful outward manner.

Thackeray.

Teach me to feel another's woe,
To hide the fault I see;
That mercy I to others show,
That mercy show to me.

Pope.

"The Persians say of noisy, unreasonable talk: 'I hear the noise of the mill-stone, but I see no meal.'"

We give advice by the bucket, but take it by the grain.

Alger.

It is much easier to be critical than correct.

Beaconsfield.

"'I am busy, Johnnie, and can't help it,' said the father, writing away when the little fellow hurt his finger. 'Yes, you could—you might have said oh!' sobbed Johnnie. There's a Johnnie in tears inside all of us upon occasions."

Rev. W. C. Gannett.

"You cannot prevent the birds of sadness from flying over your head, but you may prevent them from stopping to build their nests there."

In general society one should always avoid discussions upon two subjects—religion and politics. In a discussion upon either of these subjects you will find very little intellectual honesty, and it will almost invariably lead to irritating differences of opinion.

A gentleman is one who understands and shows every mark of deference to the claims of self-love in others and exacts it in return from them.

Hazlitt.

"There is no real conflict between truth and politeness; what is imagined to be such is only the crude mistake of those who fail to discover their harmony. Politeness, taken in its best sense, is the graceful expression of respect, kind feeling, and good will."

"Beloved among women is she who, having warned a friend of the consequences to follow rash doings, will, when her prophecies have come true, withhold the triumphant: I told you so!"

Boston Journal.

"No one loses by politeness to, or by the trifling exercise of apparent pleasure in a caller. While I have no wish to counsel insincerity, there is a wide difference between that offensive veneer and the pure metal of consideration for the feelings of a stranger within one's gate."

LADY BELLAIR'S ADVICE TO GIRLS.

WHAT TO AVOID.

A loud, weak, affected, whining, harsh or shrill tone of voice. Extravagances in conversation—such phrases as "Awfully this," "Beastly that," "Loads of time," "Don't you know," "Hate" for "dislike," etc.

Sudden exclamations of annoyance, surprise and joy,—often dangerously approaching to "female swearing"—as "Bother!" "Gracious!" "How jolly!"

Yawning when listening to anyone.

Talking on family matters, even to bosom friends.

Attempting any vocal or instrumental piece of music that you cannot execute with ease.

Crossing your letters.

Making a sharp, short nod with the head, intended to do duty as a bow.

WHAT TO CULTIVATE.

An unaffected, low, distinct, silver-toned voice.

The art of pleasing those around you, and seeming pleased with them and all they may do for you.

The charm of making little sacrifices quite naturally, as if of no account to yourself.

The habit of making allowances for the opinions, feelings, or prejudices of others.

An erect carriage—that is, a sound body.

A good memory for faces, and facts connected with them—thus avoiding giving offence through not recognizing or bowing to people, or saying to them what had best been left unsaid.

The art of listening without impatience to prosy talkers, and smiling at the twice-told tale or joke.

"He who would see his sons and daughters thoroughly and truly gentle, must forbid selfishness of action, rudeness of speech, carelessness of forms, impoliteness of conduct from the first, and demand that in childhood and the nursery shall be laid the foundation of that good breeding which is as a jewel of price to the mature man and woman."

"Many persons consider that 'bad temper' is entirely voluntary on the part of the person who displays it. As a matter of fact it is often, to a very great extent, involuntary, and no one is more angry at it than the bad tempered person himself. Of course everyone, whether he is born with a bad temper or has acquired one from habit, or has been visited with one as the result of disease or injury, should at least try to control it. But his friends should also bear in mind that bad temper may be, and often is, an affliction to be sympathized with, not an offence to be punished."

Once A Week.

There are some people so given over to the pettiness of fault-picking, that if they should suddenly see the handwriting on the wall, they would disregard its awful warning in their eager haste to point out its defective penmanship.

Brander Matthews.

"We are all dissatisfied. The only difference is that some of us sit down in the squalor of our dissatisfaction, while others make a ladder of it."

Mrs. Julia Ward Howe said, in speaking of Longfellow, that "his personal charm was in a delicateness of mind that was truly cosmopolitan; he had a vivid appreciation of what was beautiful and noble, and he represented the purest taste and the most perfect feeling." Was there ever given a finer definition of a gentleman?

"Set a watch over thy mouth, and keep the door of thy lips, for a tale-bearer is worse than a thief."

The Bible.

"He submits to be seen through a microscope who suffers himself to be caught in a passion."

"It isn't what you wear in this life, gentlemen; it is how you wear it. It isn't so much what you do; it is how you do it. There are people who do tasteful things vulgarly, and vulgar things tastefully. Who was it that

'Kicked them downstairs with such very fine grace,
They thought he was handing them up'?

"A sense of humor is one of the most precious gifts that can be vouchsafed to a human being. He is not necessarily a better man for having it, but he is a happier one. It renders him indifferent to good or bad fortune. It enables him to enjoy his own discomfiture. Blessed with this sense, he is never unduly elated or cast down. No one can ruffle his temper. No abuse disturbs his equanimity. Bores do not bore him. Humbugs do not humbug him. Solemn airs do not impose on him. Sentimental gush does not influence him. The follies of the moment have no hold on him."

Boston Journal.

There is always a best way of doing everything, if it be but to boil an egg. Manners are the happy way of doing things; each one the stroke of genius or of love—now repeated and hardened into usage. Your manners are always under examination, and by committees little suspected—a police in citizen's clothes—but are awarding or denying you very high prizes when you least think of it.

Emerson.

My experience of life makes me sure of one truth, which I do not try to explain; that the sweetest happiness we ever know, the very wine of human life, comes not from love, but from sacrifice—from the effort to make others happy. This is as true to me as that my flesh will burn if I touch red-hot metal.

John Boyle O'Reilly.

"A wise man will turn adverse criticism and malicious attacks to good account. He will consider carefully whether there is not in him some weakness or fault which, although he never discovered, was plain to the eye of his enemy. Many men profit more by the assaults of foes than by the kindness of friends."

"Politeness is like an air cushion: there may be nothing in it, but it eases our jolts wonderfully."

Don't flatter yourself that friendship authorizes you to say disagreeable things to your intimates. On the contrary, the nearer you come into relation with a person the more necessary do tact and courtesy become. Except in cases of necessity, which are rare, leave your friend to learn unpleasant truths from his enemies: they are ready enough to tell them. Good breeding never forgets that *amour-propre* is universal.

O. W. Holmes.

Whatever our disbeliefs, most of us profoundly believe in goodness; and we incline to believe that a man who has practically learned the secret of noble living has somehow got near the truth of things.

Geo. S. Merriam.

"A man's bad temper sometimes does more toward spoiling a dinner than a woman's bad cooking."

Her voice was ever soft,
Gentle and low; an excellent thing in
Woman.

Shakespeare.

True politeness is perfect ease and freedom. It simply consists in treating others just as you love to be treated yourself.

Chesterfield.

A man has no more right to say an uncivil thing than to act one, no more right to say a rude thing to another than to knock him down.

Johnson.

How sweet and gracious, even in common speech,
Is that fine sense which men call courtesy!
Wholesome as air and genial as the light,
Welcome in every clime as breath of flowers,——
It transmutes aliens into trusting friends,
And gives its owner passport round the globe.

J. T. Fields.

THE END.

www.ingramcontent.com/pod-product-compliance
Lightning Source LLC
LaVergne TN
LVHW020639100826
845148LV00012B/2246

* 9 7 8 1 7 7 0 8 3 1 4 7 6 *